Testing the Creditcoin Blockchain

A Daily Account from a Test Engineer's Perspective

Alexander Todorov

Testing the Creditcoin Blockchain: A Daily Account from a Test Engineer's Perspective

Alexander Todorov
Sofia, Sofiya, Bulgaria

ISBN-13 (pbk): 979-8-8688-0872-2   ISBN-13 (electronic): 979-8-8688-0873-9
https://doi.org/10.1007/979-8-8688-0873-9

Copyright © 2024 by The Editor(s) (if applicable) and The Author(s), under exclusive license to APress Media, LLC, part of Springer Nature

This work is subject to copyright. All rights are reserved by the Publisher, whether the whole or part of the material is concerned, specifically the rights of translation, reprinting, reuse of illustrations, recitation, broadcasting, reproduction on microfilms or in any other physical way, and transmission or information storage and retrieval, electronic adaptation, computer software, or by similar or dissimilar methodology now known or hereafter developed.

Trademarked names, logos, and images may appear in this book. Rather than use a trademark symbol with every occurrence of a trademarked name, logo, or image we use the names, logos, and images only in an editorial fashion and to the benefit of the trademark owner, with no intention of infringement of the trademark.

The use in this publication of trade names, trademarks, service marks, and similar terms, even if they are not identified as such, is not to be taken as an expression of opinion as to whether or not they are subject to proprietary rights.

While the advice and information in this book are believed to be true and accurate at the date of publication, neither the authors nor the editors nor the publisher can accept any legal responsibility for any errors or omissions that may be made. The publisher makes no warranty, express or implied, with respect to the material contained herein.

>Managing Director, Apress Media LLC: Welmoed Spahr
>Acquisitions Editor: Malini Rajendran
>Desk Editor: James Markham
>Editorial Project Manager: Gryffin Winkler

Cover image designed by Freepik (www.freepik.com)

Distributed to the book trade worldwide by Springer Science+Business Media New York, 1 New York Plaza, Suite 4600, New York, NY 10004-1562, USA. Phone 1-800-SPRINGER, fax (201) 348-4505, e-mail orders-ny@springer-sbm.com, or visit www.springeronline.com. Apress Media, LLC is a California LLC and the sole member (owner) is Springer Science + Business Media Finance Inc (SSBM Finance Inc). SSBM Finance Inc is a **Delaware** corporation.

For information on translations, please e-mail booktranslations@springernature.com; for reprint, paperback, or audio rights, please e-mail bookpermissions@springernature.com.

Apress titles may be purchased in bulk for academic, corporate, or promotional use. eBook versions and licenses are also available for most titles. For more information, reference our Print and eBook Bulk Sales web page at http://www.apress.com/bulk-sales.

Any source code or other supplementary material referenced by the author in this book is available to readers on GitHub. For more detailed information, please visit https://www.apress.com/gp/services/source-code.

If disposing of this product, please recycle the paper

To the tester who gave me everything.

You showed me what true, unconditional love and sacrifice is. I will always cherish the time that you allowed me to be together with you!

I am deeply sorry that I was too selfish to not realize it in time. I apologize from the bottom of my heart that I hurt and betrayed you by taking away your most sacred dream.

Please forgive me!

Table of Contents

About the Author xi

About the Technical Reviewer xiii

Acknowledgments xv

Preface xvii

Part I: Introduction to Blockchain 1

Chapter 1: Introduction 3

    Introduction to Blockchain 4

    Blockchain Attributes 6

    Blockchain Glossary 8

    Blockchain Components 17

        Peer-to-Peer Networking 19

        Consensus Algorithm 19

        Transactions 20

        Transaction Fees 21

        Block Production 21

        Block Rewards 22

        Remote Procedure Call (RPC) API 22

        Storage 23

        Migrations 24

        Runtime Upgrades 24

        Metrics and Telemetry 25

TABLE OF CONTENTS

Off-Chain Worker or Oracle 25
Smart Contracts 25
Consensus Mechanisms 26
Proof of Work (PoW) 27
Proof of Stake (PoS) 27
Proof of Authority (PoA) 28
Summary 28

Chapter 2: Blockchain Development Frameworks 29

Hyperledger Sawtooth 29
Substrate 30
Ethereum 31
Programming Languages 31
How Do You Build a Blockchain Implementation 35
Thoughts on Development and Testing 38
Summary 40

Part II: The Creditcoin Blockchain: Aims and Objectives 41

Chapter 3: Introducing the Creditcoin Blockchain 43

What Is Creditcoin 43
Impact on Testing Activities 47
Summary 50

Part III: Testing the Creditcoin Blockchain 51

Chapter 4: Creditcoin 1.x 53

Components of Creditcoin 1.x 55
Client 55
Validator 56
Consensus 57

TABLE OF CONTENTS

    Transaction Processor(s) 58

    REST API 59

    Gateway 60

    SDKs 61

    Creditcoin-Legacy-Tests 61

    Creditcoin-Legacy-Docker-Compose 62

    Creditcoin-Legacy-Docker-Compose-Testnet 62

Timeline of Creditcoin 1.x 62

Testing Creditcoin 1.x 63

    State of Testing Before I Joined 66

    Testing Overview 66

    Improvement on Tests 69

    Testing v1.7 ➤ v1.8 Switchover and Suspected Networking Issues 74

The End 75

Summary 76

Chapter 5: Creditcoin 2.0 79

Components of Creditcoin 2.0 81

    Extrinsics Pallets 83

    Transaction Fees 85

    Weights and Benchmarks 86

    Runtime 86

    Storage Migrations 87

    Custom RPCs 88

    Telemetry and Custom Metrics 88

    Creditcoin-js 89

    Creditcoin-squid 89

TABLE OF CONTENTS

Timeline of Creditcoin 2.0 90
Testing of Creditcoin 2.0 91
    Unit Testing 93
    Integration Testing 98
    Sanity Testing and Static Analysis 102
    Testing with Bots 104
    Migrations and Upgrade Testing 106
    Continuous Testing on Pull Requests, Devnet, Testnet, and Mainnet 112
    Security-Related Testing 118
    Testing Creditcoin-squid 120
    How We Found a Bug at Block 1 Million 120
    Other Interesting Facts 121
Summary 124

Chapter 6: Creditcoin 2.3 125
Components of Creditcoin 2.3 126
    Staking-Related Pallets 126
    Creditcoin-cli 126
    Switch_to_pos() 127
    Block History 129
    Creditcoin Staking Dashboard 129
    Subscan Essentials 130
    Creditcoin-squid 130
Timeline of Creditcoin 2.3 130
Testing of Creditcoin 2.3 131
    Unit Tests 131
    Integration Tests 132
    Testing Subscan Essentials 134
    Testing Creditcoin Staking Dashboard 135

TABLE OF CONTENTS

 Testing Creditcoin-cli 136

 Testing Gluwa's Substrate Fork 138

 Community Testing on PoS Testnet 140

 Documentation Review 144

 Load and Performance Testing 145

 Security Bounty Program 147

 Other Interesting Testing and Some Bugs 149

Testing Challenges During v2.3 154

Migration from PoW to PoS 157

Summary 157

Chapter 7: Creditcoin 3.0 159

Components of Creditcoin 3.0 160

 Polkadot-sdk 160

 Frontier 161

 Creditcoin3 162

 EVM Tracing RPC 162

 Precompile(s) 163

 Creditcoin 3 CLI 164

 Proxy Functionality 164

 Staking Dashboard 166

 Subscan API 167

 Blockscout 167

 Crunch 168

Timeline of Creditcoin 3.0 168

Testing of Creditcoin 3.0 168

 Unit Tests 169

 EVM and Smart-Contract Testing 170

 Testing EVM Tracing Functionality 171

ix

TABLE OF CONTENTS

    Integration Tests for the Blockchain 172

    Precompile Testing 173

    Testing Creditcoin 3 CLI and Proxy Functionality 174

    Runtime Upgrade Testing 185

    Testing Creditcoin Staking Dashboard 185

    Testing Gluwa's Polkadot-sdk Fork 189

    Testing Gluwa's Frontier Fork 189

    Testing Gluwa's Crunch Fork 190

    Documentation Review and Third-Party Tools Testing 190

    Other Interesting Testing 192

  Summary 206

Part IV: Blockchain Testing Approaches 207

Chapter 8: How Others Test Blockchain 209

  My Blockchain Testing Approach 209

  Testing Across the Blockchain Stack with Andrew Snaith 211

    Products Under Test 212

    Testing Strategy 214

  Testing Smart Contracts with Sebastian Viquez 222

    Product Under Test 223

    Testing 226

  Summary 241

Index 243

About the Author

Alexander Todorov is a quality assurance engineer and an ISTQB and Red Hat certified professional with two decades of industry experience, an open source hacker with thousands of contributions, a Python instructor, and co-organizer of FOSDEM's Testing and Continuous Delivery devroom. He's also tested multiple components of Red Hat Enterprise Linux, was a test lead for the entire lifecycle of its version 5 family, and later tested various components of the Creditcoin blockchain.

Alex holds a master's degree in Computer Engineering from the Technical University of Sofia, Bulgaria, and loves public speaking and riding fast motorcycles. In his spare time, he's the lead engineer behind Kiwi TCMS, a popular open source test management system.

You can find Alex on LinkedIn, https://www.linkedin.com/in/alextodorov/, and follow his work directly on GitHub via https://github.com/atodorov.

About the Technical Reviewer

Anandaganesh Balakrishnan is a data engineering and data analytics leader who has held senior leadership roles across the fintech, biotech, and utility domains. His expertise is architecting scalable, reliable, and performant data platforms for advanced data analytics, quantitative research, and machine learning. His current research is AI on unstructured data, large language models (LLMs), generative AI (Gen AI), self-service data analytics, and data catalogs.

Acknowledgments

I want to thank Jeroen Rosink for being the first one who gave me feedback about the contents of this book. You've given me valuable feedback several times till now. I may have misunderstood some of it and definitely not incorporated everything, but I have no doubt that your feedback has made a positive difference on my end.

Next round of thanks goes to Sebastian Malyska who helped me get in touch with other blockchain testers. Seba, I hope we meet soon at another testing conference!

Thank you to my fellow tester and neighbor Liviu Damian for putting me in touch with Andrew Snaith.

Thank you Andrew Snaith for agreeing to share your testing experience for this book which added many other dimensions to my personal stories.

Last but not least, thank you Sebastian Viquez for agreeing to share your testing experience around smart contracts which completes this book.

Preface

This book follows the quality engineering journey of the Creditcoin blockchain across four distinct implementation versions and a myriad of technologies from a first-person point of view. It discusses testing implementations with the Hyperledger Sawtooth and Substrate blockchain frameworks, testing switch from proof-of-work to proof-of-stake consensus algorithm and testing an Ethereum Virtual Machine compatibility layer.

Readers will traverse several years of fast-paced blockchain implementations and technological changes including explanation of all major components under test, the approach taken, including examples of test automation and tools, interesting bugs, and testing challenges. Chapters follow each major implementation of the Creditcoin blockchain and conclude with a couple interviews with other testers working on different blockchain-related products.

Almost 99% of everything discussed in this book is open source, and multiple references to source code and GitHub are included throughout.

This book is for the software tester and quality engineering folks, who may soon be working on a blockchain implementation without having the necessary understanding of what it is, how it works, and what is important in terms of "assuring" quality.

Target audience:

- Software tester
- Software developer in test automation
- Quality assurance engineer
- Quality assurance manager

PREFACE

What you will learn:

1. Key components of a blockchain with some diagrams
2. Glossary of popular blockchain and crypto terms
3. Overview of blockchain implementation with the Hyperledger Sawtooth framework
4. Overview of blockchain implementation with the Substrate framework
5. Practical topics related to testing proof-of-work, proof-of-stake, and EVM-based blockchains

PART I

Introduction to Blockchain

CHAPTER 1

Introduction

Cryptographer David Chaum first proposed a blockchain-like protocol in his 1982 dissertation "Computer Systems Established, Maintained, and Trusted by Mutually Suspicious Groups" with further improvements on this idea in the next 15–20 years.

The first decentralized blockchain was conceptualized by a person (or group of people) known as Satoshi Nakamoto in 2008 giving rise to Bitcoin. 2013 was the start of Ethereum which introduced smart contract functionality. Due to concerns over the high energy consumption required for cryptographic computations, later chains such as Cardano (2017), Solana (2020), and Polkadot (2020) started adopting the less energy-intensive proof-of-stake model.

At present, we are witnessing continuously increasing interest and investment into blockchain technology[1] with a multitude of companies searching for practical applications beyond cryptocurrencies. It is the time when blockchain technology is entering the world of the more common software engineering folks. It is also the time when blockchain technology is being productized, which leads to the necessity of more testing for these products.

As an experienced quality assurance engineer with nearly two decades of experience, I felt very intrigued about working in the blockchain testing space, yet at the same time, I felt extremely uncomfortable for a very long time. I've had prior experience with testing low-level infrastructure type

---

[1] https://www.statista.com/topics/5122/blockchain/#statisticChapter

© The Editor(s) (if applicable) and The Author(s),
under exclusive license to APress Media, LLC, part of Springer Nature 2024
A. Todorov, *Testing the Creditcoin Blockchain*, https://doi.org/10.1007/979-8-8688-0873-9_1

of software, like various parts of the Linux operating system, but didn't have any experience with cryptocurrency or blockchain before. Because I was working on a product that was already in production, I needed to learn a lot of things very quickly in order to be a productive member of the team. It was like drinking from a firehose, and to this day it feels like that sometimes.

This book is for the common tester and quality engineering folks, who may very soon be required to work on a blockchain software product without having the necessary understanding of what it is, how it actually works, and what is important in terms of "assuring" quality.

Blockchain networks are distributed systems which are usually more complex compared to regular software products, and there are a myriad of items to be tested which requires a vast skill set. This book is not meant to be an exhaustive resource for every possible scenario; that is impossible. Instead, it is meant to tell my story as a blockchain test engineer and hopefully be your starting point in this domain.

Happy testing!

Introduction to Blockchain

There are multiple components in distributed systems like blockchain, and some of them are not necessarily common knowledge unless you have worked in this specific technical field before. This chapter explains what a blockchain is and establishes some of the common terms used in this domain and gives you some examples.

A blockchain is a growing list of records, called blocks, which are securely linked together by cryptographic functions which guarantee that data is tamper proof. In the context of Figure 1-1, we can think about each block as a snapshot of the current state at a specific period of time. If someone tries to modify this state at a later date, that would cause all of the blocks afterward to be invalid with respect to the modified block, thus revealing data tampering. It is also referred to as a distributed digital ledger. Such architecture allows for participants who don't trust each other to still have trust in the data recorded onto the blockchain.

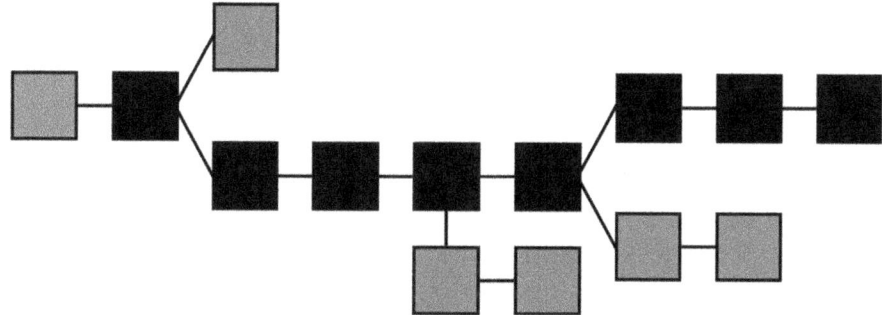

Figure 1-1. *Example of linked data blocks forming a blockchain License: CC BY 3.0, source* `https://commons.wikimedia.org/wiki/File:Blockchain_landscape.svg`

Blockchain participants are individual operators who execute the blockchain client software on their computer systems. Their motivation is usually financial – to gain rewards for providing distributed computing resources to the blockchain.

In order to record new information onto the blockchain, participants must be in agreement – for example, what is the answer to a difficult mathematical problem. This is known as consensus. By design, most blockchain systems are open for participation to anyone, and in many cases participants are anonymous, could be faulty (due to software or hardware bugs) or misbehaving (due to possible external incentive to falsify records in the blockchain), and generally cannot be trusted. It is the job of a consensus algorithm to ensure that participants in such a system can reach an agreement and to detect and exclude participants who are considered to be at fault. Otherwise, the blockchain software cannot proceed to the next step, which is recording actual data into storage.

CHAPTER 1   INTRODUCTION

Once new transactions are combined into a block and this block is distributed across multiple nodes in the blockchain, it cannot be erased or modified. The blockchain ensures full transaction history, and the use of cryptographic functions ensures that information recorded on the chain is secure by design. These records are essentially read-only. Algorithms and software architecture are chosen so that they guarantee these principles. The actual cryptographic, consensus, networking, and other algorithms and implementation architectures vary, and there is a lot of ongoing research in this space, but the underlying principle is ensuring data integrity as shown in Figure 1-1.

Although many of today's blockchain platforms are capable of supporting smart contracts and cryptocurrencies, these are not strictly required for the core operation of a blockchain as a secure distributed ledger. It is the opposite, being a secure distributed ledger, that makes the existence of smart contracts and cryptocurrencies possible.

A blockchain implementation is an infrastructure type of software which on a very high abstraction level resembles a database – there is some data recorded in storage and the outside world, that is, other applications can read and write to the blockchain.

Blockchain applications are usually more complex than other pieces of software that testers may be familiar with, with multiple components working in parallel and multiple networking channels and protocols being active at the same time.

Blockchain Attributes

This section is included only for your reference. In a practical implementation, most of these attributes are available to you out of the box, courtesy of the chosen blockchain framework.

CHAPTER 1   INTRODUCTION

The testing requirements around these particular attributes depend on your operational and business requirements and in practical implementations, for example, where you are not developing the underlying algorithms themselves, are most likely going to be resolved by having heavy monitoring and alerts rather than a functional test suite.

- **Security**: Information on a blockchain is generally considered to be secure against modification so that historical records can be trusted. The blockchain is also considered generally secure against malicious actors because of its distributed nature

- **Fault tolerance**: In a blockchain network, there may be nodes which exhibit faulty behavior or are downright malicious. Blockchain implementations have built-in tolerance against this.

- **Reliability**: The probability that the blockchain will work properly in a specified environment and for a given amount of time. For nominated proof-of-stake consensus, this translates to having at least two-thirds of all elected validators online and functioning properly during the current era.

- **Reproducibility**: Transactions on the blockchain can be replayed by another node which should always result in the same state, for example, same information stored locally on disk for the node replaying the transactions.

- **Transparency**: Records on a public blockchain are accessible to everyone, and all state transitions, from genesis to the current block, can be replayed and verified individually. That is, even though participants are generally anonymous, all of their actions are fully transparent and can be retraced by anyone.

CHAPTER 1   INTRODUCTION

- **Finality** is the level of confidence that a well-formed block recently appended to the blockchain will not be revoked in the future and thus can be trusted. Most distributed blockchain protocols cannot guarantee the finality of a freshly committed block, and instead rely on "probabilistic finality": as the block goes deeper into a blockchain, it is less likely to be altered or reverted by a newly found consensus.

- **Public vs. private**: Whether the blockchain is fully open to the public, for example, anyone can participate or not. Blockchains that you hear about in the news are public, including Creditcoin.

- **Permissionless vs. permissioned**: Whether anyone can join an existing blockchain network, operate a node, and participate in consensus with/without first obtaining some sort of permission, approval, etc. Popular blockchains like Bitcoin, Ethereum, and, of course, Creditcoin are permissionless.

Blockchain Glossary

Transaction much like in a regular SQL database is an operation that seeks to append new information onto the blockchain. It is usually exposed as an API function so that users may interact with the blockchain. Blockchain transactions are usually a singular entity analogous to a single SQL statement executed against a traditional database. Transactions represent the blockchain's business domain, for example, `AddBidOrder` for Creditcoin or transfer of Ether from one party to another in the case of Ethereum. There can be multiple transaction types supported by a blockchain network.

CHAPTER 1   INTRODUCTION

A **hash** is the result of a one-way cryptographic function usually receiving binary data as input and returning a hexadecimal string! Each data has a unique hash representation, and you cannot reverse the hash value back to the original input data. Even a one-bit modification of the input data will result in vastly different hash value. This makes it safe to publicly share the hash value in lieu of the data itself and to use the same hash value to verify that two pieces of data are exactly the same thing.

Transaction hash is a hexadecimal string representing the cryptographic hash of each transaction. Very often these strings are used in lieu of identifiers. For example, `https://etherscan.io/tx/0x8d116ea41628ac89745c95147c0ea394809074607395b0d792d1bea9136280b1` represents a transaction where I have exchanged one crypto token (G-CRE) for another (ETH).

Gas or **transaction fee** is the representation of how much it costs to execute a particular transaction on the blockchain. It can vary over time and between transaction types and is meant to represent the computational expense for the transaction. This value is usually represented by the blockchain's native crypto token. The purpose of gas is related to token economics and also provides a security feature making malicious behavior economically not viable.

A **block explorer** is typically a web application which allows the user to search and inspect blocks, transactions, and addresses on a blockchain. A popular one is Etherscan linked in the previous paragraph. For Creditcoin, a similar function is performed by Subscan (`https://creditcoin3-testnet.subscan.io/`) and Blockscout (`https://creditcoin-testnet.blockscout.com`).

Block is a collection of multiple transactions that are recorded atomically onto the blockchain. Either all transactions within the block are recorded together or none of them are. If we make an analogy with the git version control system, a single chunk of modified source code will be a *"transaction,"* while a git commit of multiple modifications will be "the *block*."

9

CHAPTER 1   INTRODUCTION

While we may commonly refer to blocks as records, the meaning is different compared to a database record, which represents a singular collection of discrete values, in other words a row of column values. In the blockchain context, the term record is closer in meaning to the vinyl disk record which holds multiple songs.

Blocks contain a list of transactions, references to the previous and next blocks, as well as additional metadata such as time stamps, cryptographic hashes, and signatures. There is a maximum limit of how many transactions can be stored in a single block, depending on implementation.

Block fullness or **block saturation** level represents the percentage of how much of the total available space within a block is actually used. For example, if the blockchain is not in use, each block may hold a single heartbeat/timestamp transaction. Or it may hold hundreds of transactions in a heavily used blockchain.

Block hash is the hexadecimal string representing the cryptographic hash of each block. Very often these strings are used in lieu of addresses or identifiers. For example, 0x34e89f72d1bc09af19759a94c347d769a94bb0 ca9d257b2efe8ad5ac0502cc11 corresponds to block number 19517842 on the Ethereum main network. Its contents can be inspected via https://etherscan.io/block/0x34e89f72d1bc09af19759a94c34 7d769a94bb0ca9d257b2efe8ad5ac0502cc11 or https://etherscan. io/block/19517842. This block contains 185 individual transactions, including the one where I have swapped some tokens.

Block height or **block number** is the number of blocks preceding it. Older blocks have lower height. The bigger this number, the longer the blockchain has been in existence.

Block time is the average time between blocks on the blockchain, for example, 15 seconds. The value itself is arbitrary and is chosen by the creators of the blockchain. The important thing is that this value is approximately a constant. In Bitcoin, the expected block time is 10 minutes, while in Ethereum the design calls for a block time of

15 seconds which in practice is usually between 10 and 19 seconds. Initial implementations of Creditcoin used 60 seconds, with later versions dropping down to 15 seconds. Constant block time is better for layered applications because they can know in what timeframe an operation can be considered as failed or timed out.

Genesis block is block number zero. It is usually hard-coded into the blockchain implementation, for example, your client program, and may contain metadata that's necessary for the subsequent correct operation of the chain. For example, which account is the root account or a starting balance for a set of predefined addresses.

A **fork** happens when the blockchain diverges into two potential paths forward. A fork may occur when multiple nodes produce a block at nearly the same time. The fork is resolved when subsequent blocks are added and one of the paths becomes longer than the alternatives.

A **hard fork** usually occurs when there is a change to the blockchain protocol that is not backward-compatible and requires all users to upgrade their software in order to continue participating in the network. In a hard fork scenario, the blockchain network exists as two separate digital entities which are not connected to one another. Hard forks may also occur due to bugs in the software implementation and/or networking issues which lead to consensus failure. In other words, participants in the blockchain cannot come to an agreement which path forward should be the canonical one and the result is two separate chains.

Since a blockchain is meant to be used as a source of truth, situations in which forks cannot be resolved and the result is a hard-fork are considered to be critical and potentially damaging to the blockchain.

Block **finality** refers to the irreversible confirmation of transactions on a blockchain, ensuring security and preventing double-spending. Block **finalization** is the process used to handle forks and choose the canonical chain where the majority of the participants are in agreement that blocks should not be reverted. In practical terms, this means two-thirds of all participants.

CHAPTER 1   INTRODUCTION

State is the current snapshot on the blockchain – the total number of blocks, the transactions recorded in these blocks, and the value(s) recorded in local storage. In practice when we talk about state, we mean a snapshot of the blockchain at a specific block. For example, the state at block 1000 is that Alice has a balance of 300 and Bob has none! In block 1010, the internal state may have changed due to transactions which have been executed in the meantime. For example, Bob has now earned a certain amount of tokens. When we talk about state, quite often we mean the last values recorded onto the blockchain ignoring previous history. Depending on the context, we may want to take into account prior history, probably if you are trying to reproduce a specific bug.

Mining is the process of performing computationally intensive cryptographic operations as part of the proof-of-work consensus algorithm. Computers performing this work are known as **miners**. Broadly speaking, we also use the term **miner** when referring to a computer and/or a human participating in a blockchain, regardless of the actual consensus algorithm.

In cryptography and blockchain, a **nonce** is an arbitrary number that can be used just once in communication. It is often a pseudo-random number issued in an authentication protocol to ensure that old communications cannot be reused in replay attacks.

Validator is a computer node which verifies the legitimacy of blockchain transactions. Also known as **miners** or **minters**, validators are the ones who participate in the consensus algorithm and gain privilege to append blocks to the blockchain. The process is entirely automated, and when we say "user," we generally mean a computer participating in the blockchain network; however, keep in mind that this computer is operated by a human, aka the user, which may also be referred to with the same terms. The term validator is commonly used with proof-of-stake consensus algorithms, while miner is more commonly used with the proof-of-work algorithm.

CHAPTER 1   INTRODUCTION

A **nominator** is a participant in the blockchain which votes with their funds in favor of selected validators. In proof-of-stake networks, nominators are a role of users who can participate in the blockchain without needing much technical knowledge to operate a blockchain node. They are sometimes also known as **"investors"** because they only use their funds, as opposed to technical operators.

[Crypto] token is some sort of digital token that is used to represent value on the blockchain in order for the blockchain network to be economically sustainable. Validators are rewarded tokens in exchange for operating computing hardware that supports the blockchain and the data stored within it.

Tokens such as BTC, ETH, CTC, and others are referred to as **cryptocurrency** which then may take a life of its own. Because a token is a representation of value, it can be exchanged for other tokens of value, for example, paper money, also called **fiat currency**, or another digital token. Token economics is outside the scope of this book.

The existence of crypto tokens is usually a must for public blockchain networks because it provides the incentive for operators to join the network. Private networks with stricter access control and/or focus on solving a particular business problem would rarely need crypto tokens. The expected profit of solving the business problem at hand provides the necessary motivation for operators of such networks.

Note   Blockchains usually have what's called a **native token** or a **utility token** which is meant to facilitate operating the blockchain. Then there can be other tokens, also known as **coins**, which could be exchanged, traded, or used for any other purposes. It is not uncommon that such **coins** are attributed significant value just because of their existence, not because of their technical utility.

13

CHAPTER 1   INTRODUCTION

A [crypto] **wallet address** is represented as a long hexadecimal string which holds information about different crypto tokens and their balance owned by whoever controls it. The hex string is used as the wallet address and in practice represents the public key of a private-public key pair. In general wallets are anonymous accounts on the blockchain. Note that this address is relevant to a particular blockchain. My address on Ethereum is `0x718bb20f20ab1937710D2Ac579D97835a6fD099C`. This address may not exist on other blockchain networks. It is also important to note that different blockchains may use different address formats and representation. In Ethereum the length is **20 bytes** represented by 40 hexadecimal digits as shown above. In Creditcoin, the Substrate framework, the format is **32-byte** account identifier; however, not all addresses in Substrate-based networks are based on keys.

Since the algorithms generating these addresses have very low probability of collisions, wallet addresses are practically unique and can be used across different blockchains as long as the format is supported. In practice, the first time a transfer is made to a particular address, the "account" behind it will start to exist on that particular blockchain.

A **wallet app** is an application which holds your public/private keys and allows the user to interact with a blockchain by signing transactions for transferring or exchanging different crypto tokens. Most commonly that is a web browser extension or a mobile application. Popular wallet apps, for example, are **MetaMask** and **SubWallet**, but there are many more available with varying functionality. For example, the financial mobile application Revolut also contains features of a crypto wallet, allowing you to purchase tokens, send transfers to other addresses, or make investments in crypto, even though its feature scope is much larger. Because wallet apps hold private keys and allow the user to sign transactions, they are often one of the most visible software pieces for a user interacting with a blockchain.

Note that depending on context, the term **wallet** may refer either to the address of an account, or to the user facing application used to manipulate funds in this account or both.

CHAPTER 1   INTRODUCTION

A crypto **faucet** is a quick way of rewarding users with small amounts of crypto tokens in exchange for performing various tasks on a website or mobile application. The tasks the user completes could be clicking on a paid ad, completing a CAPTCHA test, logging in every day, or interacting with a Discord bot, for example. In a blockchain testing environment, your team will probably have internal/external faucets to help testers acquire some cryptocurrency and use it for testing.

An **airdrop** is a marketing strategy that involves sending coins or tokens to wallet addresses of active members of the blockchain community for free or in return for a small service. For testing purposes, it performs the same function as faucets but is not self-service.

Mainnet, testnet, devnet, and **stagenet** are separate instances of a blockchain network. They are isolated from one another, and you can have as many as you need for testing and development purposes. Unique accounts, tokens, blocks, and transactions will exist in each instance of the network. The instance called **mainnet** is the production environment. The rest are assigned more or less arbitrarily by the blockchain creators. Some blockchains may have multiple test and development environments denoted by names.

Staking is the action of committing a certain amount of crypto tokens in order to participate in the proof-of-stake consensus mechanism. This applies to both validator and nominator roles. The economic incentive is higher return on investment. While similar to traditional investment instruments, the process of staking by itself is meant to be a process where the user is actively engaged in order to ensure a healthy community for the blockchain. Remember that a blockchain is a highly distributed environment and the more participants the better.

Slashing is the process of applying penalties (taking away tokens) to a malicious validator in a Proof of Stake blockchain network thus making such behavior economically unviable. Slashing also extends to nominators, and that's why it is recommended for participants in blockchain staking to be active and monitor what's happening on the blockchain regularly. For example, do not vote for a validator and then forget about it.

Client program is any software program that communicates with a blockchain. In the context of a blockchain application, we usually mean the software program that is executed natively on the computer and implements the various components of the blockchain. That's typically the program which acts as a validator on the blockchain. In a broader context, a client can also refer to a wallet application or to yet another application interacting with the blockchain, for example, a staking dashboard or a telemetry dashboard. It can also mean an application designed to interact with a particular smart contract.

Some blockchain implementations have a separate **runtime** component which encapsulates the transactions and business logic while the client itself is delegated the lower level tasks of communicating over the network, writing to disk storage, consensus, etc.

Web3 is an idea for a new iteration of the World Wide Web which incorporates concepts such as decentralization, blockchain technologies, and token-based economics. The term was coined in 2014 by Ethereum co-founder Gavin Wood.

A **smart contract** is a program written in a particular programming language, for example, Solidity, and stored on a blockchain capable of executing such programs. Not all blockchains support smart contracts. The most popular example is implementing a cryptocurrency token, say stored on Ethereum mainnet; however, smart contracts are not limited to that. Examples demonstrate transactional games such as tick-tac-toe, voting, blind auctions, payment channels, and more. I think everything that can be represented as transactions can be programmed into a smart contract.

The core properties of a smart contract are that it cannot be changed once deployed on-chain (it is tied to a particular address or transaction hash) and that interactions with the smart contract are transparent, represented in the form of transactions, even though participants on all

CHAPTER 1　INTRODUCTION

sides may be anonymous and not necessarily trust each other. Smart contracts may also execute other smart contracts by calling functions exposed by them. Execution of functions defined inside a smart contract is recorded as transactions on the blockchain. Once deployed on-chain, smart contracts cannot change; however, you can deploy newer versions of the contract which results in a different contract address. Smart contracts have the concept of contract storage, aka storage, available internally to the contract which can hold information such as token balances for a newly created cryptocurrency.

EVM, or an **Ethereum Virtual Machine**, is the environment for executing smart contracts and decentralized applications. As the name suggests, this specification comes from the Ethereum mainnet blockchain. This specification is open and is maintained by the Ethereum Foundation and the Ethereum community.

Blockchain Components

Architecture diagram of single compute node for the Polygon zkEVM network is used as an illustration of complexity in blockchain implementations:

CHAPTER 1 INTRODUCTION

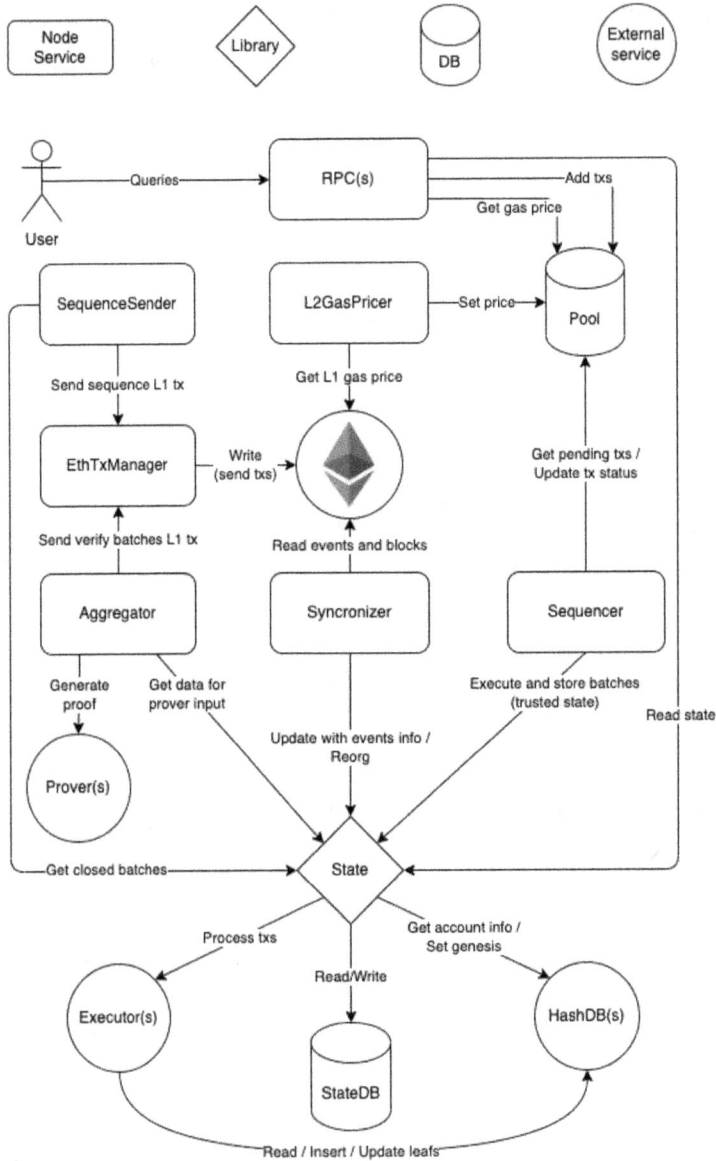

Figure 1-2. *A node in the Polygon network and its components*
Source: *https://github.com/0xPolygonHermez/zkevm-node#architecture*
License: *GNU AFFERO GENERAL PUBLIC LICENSE, Version 3*

Blockchain applications have multiple components working in parallel with one another and working in a distributed fashion. All of these components can be viewed as a separate software system, for example, peer-to-peer networking, with their own modules, complexities, and testing requirements. A lot of these components rely on algorithms which aren't used in other more common software development areas. Thus blockchain implementations tend to be more complex than other pieces of software.

Peer-to-Peer Networking

Blockchain nodes need to communicate with one another for the purposes of exchanging data and information about the network, for example, blocks. This happens over a peer-to-peer network.

This component is responsible for peer discovery and connections management. It is some sort of a peer-to-peer networking implementation, for example, based on the libp2p library. There may be other components which need or communicate over a network, and they can be separate from one another, for example, exposed via a different TCP port or implemented as a different stand-alone process.

Consensus Algorithm

A fundamental problem in distributed computing systems is to achieve overall system reliability in the presence of a number of faulty nodes or untrusted nodes. This often requires coordinating processes to agree on some data value that is needed during computation.

The consensus algorithm, consensus model, or consensus engine ensures that participants in the blockchain agree on the current state of the blockchain and are designed to secure the blockchain by preventing malicious participants from gaining an opportunity to append blocks in the chain.

CHAPTER 1   INTRODUCTION

Transactions

Aside from the actual mechanism of serializing a singular transaction into binary format so that it can be recorded into a block, the transactions component of a blockchain represents its business logic. That is, what kind of operations may be recorded on this particular blockchain.

For example, money transfer (as the original concept behind modern blockchain), insurance, lending, and borrowing in the case of Creditcoin and generally anything related to financial assets, logistics and supply chain tracking, proof and transfer of ownership (e.g., real estate deeds), etc.

An example which is practical yet simple to understand is the Tic-Tac-Toe game. We may have transactions to record the start of a new game, record each player's turn (e.g., symbol and position on the board), and the final outcome of the game. A transaction schema may look like this:

- start_game(player_one_address, player_two_address)
- record_move(player_address, symbol, coordinates_on_board)
- calculate_outcome() - may be triggered internally
- record_victory(player_address)

In the case of the original Creditcoin whitepaper, a transaction schema looks like this:

- Borrower asks for a loan (specific-terms).
- Lender proposes a loan (specific-terms).
- Record a Lender and Borrower pair, e.g., terms match/they agree on terms.
- Record transfer of funds.
- Actual transfer of funds, etc.

Transactions may be consumed internally between nodes in the blockchain – for example, each Tic-Tac-Toe participant is required to be a validator on the blockchain and can only communicate with the blockchain via their validator program.

It is however more practical that transactions are also exposed externally and are available via some sort of RPC interface. This means players in the game may be different from validators. This also means they can participate more easily, for example, via mobile or a web application, while utilizing the blockchain to record their actions.

Transaction Fees

The operation and maintenance of a blockchain network is not free of charge. It requires real-world computing resources which are often contributed by a large external community. This is especially true in public blockchain networks. This requires introducing transaction fees in the form of crypto tokens.

In order to make the blockchain economically flexible, it is necessary that the implementation controls the transaction fee component according to its needs. It could be a simple mathematical formula, or it can be a more complex algorithm taking multiple factors into account, including but not limited to historical performance on the blockchain. For example, when the usage is high and it's trending upward, then fees can rise as well. If the network has been idle for some period of time, fees can automatically adjust downward in order to stimulate more usage.

Block Production

This is a component responsible for serializing transactions into a block and communicating with the consensus, storage, and peer-to-peer components. It is important that a blockchain is able to produce new blocks. If there is no external activity, then a `time.set` transaction may be triggered by an internal clock.

Block production can be compromised due to software bugs in this component or because of consensus or networking issues. When the blockchain cannot recover, it is said that **we brick the blockchain** and the chain becomes unusable, that is, no more blocks can be appended to it and that most likely will mean the end of your blockchain.

Block Rewards

Miners and/or validators on a blockchain will usually expect to earn rewards in exchange for them providing computing resources to maintain the infrastructure.

Similar to transaction fees, rewards are represented as crypto tokens (could be the same or different), and usually they can be adjustable. The block rewards component could be a simple mathematical formula or a more complex algorithm – this is up to the creators of a particular blockchain to decide.

This formula may change over time depending on the popularity of a blockchain, e.g., higher rewards during initial phases to stimulate participation and then scale down the rewards as the blockchain becomes more popular or saturated with participants.

Remote Procedure Call (RPC) API

In order for blockchain users to be able to interact with the network, they need some sort of network-enabled interface. The RPC component is responsible for how RPC methods are defined inside a blockchain implementation and how they are exposed to the outside world. When talking about "users," here I mean "API consumers" regardless of their role in real life.

For example, serve the API interface via the JSON-RPC and/or REST protocols which may be exposed via HTTP and/or WebSocket. Other network transport and RPC protocols may also be used in various implementations. For example, the Hyperledger Sawtooth blockchain framework uses ZeroMQ/Protobuf as its internal communication layer which if I'm not mistaken clients can use directly. For the purposes of convenience, this layer is wrapped into REST API.

The most important component which needs to be exported via an RPC layer is the transaction interface. Exposing the transactions API via standard network protocols allows multiple types of applications to be able to interact with the blockchain. Using widely adopted industry protocols makes it easier to access this API from any sort of programming language.

For example, a mobile application may be signing transactions with a public-private key pair and sending them to a blockchain node, which in turn will communicate this transaction to other nodes on the p2p network and the transaction will eventually be included into a block. The node receiving the transaction via the RPC API component may be different from the node performing validation and block production.

Storage

Responsible for persisting data locally on disk at each node participating in the network, typically as a highly efficient key-value store.

For practical development purposes, the data represented on the blockchain must be represented via data types which have fields, rather than a stream of binary blobs. That is, we have a data schema which is used during the development of the blockchain software program and could also be used by third parties in the form of an SDK.

For the purposes of abstraction, parts of the storage component may be viewed as an Object Relational Mapping framework commonly found in web application development.

CHAPTER 1   INTRODUCTION

Migrations

In order for practical blockchain applications to evolve according to business needs, developers need to be able to modify the data schema. For example, in our Tic-Tac-Toe example, we may want to record in which move a game was won, or we may want to allow a third player.

Similar to ORM frameworks, the migration component allows developers to transform the data represented onto a blockchain, or even remove some of it. All of these transformations will be kept in the blockchain history at a particular block height. Older data may be retrieved if querying older blocks, but there is no guarantee for client applications to be backward compatible.

Failed migrations could lead to compromised block production which may be fatal.

Runtime Upgrades

Originating from the need of blockchain applications to evolve due to business needs, there will be different versions of the implementation. Let's say that we want to introduce the ability for three players to compete simultaneously against one another in our Tic-Tac-Toe blockchain.

The runtime upgrade component is responsible for that. In some blockchain implementations, the business logic (transactions) may be kept separately from the actual client program. This is the case when using the Substrate blockchain framework. A popular choice is the WebAssembly format. If the runtime is separate, it could also be recorded onto the blockchain itself.

In other implementations, the transactions may be tightly coupled with the rest of the client program requiring a software upgrade and restart before the user can access newer features of the blockchain.

This component raises questions around compatibility/interoperability testing between different clients and runtime versions.

Metrics and Telemetry

Since blockchain applications are distributed and the participation of a high number of nodes is encouraged for security reasons, it is often necessary to expose information about the inner workings of the blockchain software. These could be aggregated into a tool such as Grafana for further analysis.

The telemetry component is where such metrics can be defined and then pushed to external services via HTTP, for example.

Off-Chain Worker or Oracle

In the context of blockchain, all computations and state are stored onto the chain itself. Practical applications however need to communicate with the outside world and securely transfer information in and out of the blockchain. This is the domain of the so-called oracle or off-chain worker component.

An important note here is that the off-chain worker would be able to read on-chain data but should not be able to modify it directly. This component will be sending transactions back to the blockchain though if it needs to reflect the state of the outside world. This could happen internally, for example, call the transaction function in the source code or routed externally to the blockchain via the existing RPC interface. These transaction calls will then be processed by the rest of the components and if successful will make it into a block. It is also possible that a transaction will fail and/or not make it into a block for various reasons.

Smart Contracts

Smart contracts are computer programs stored onto a blockchain network. Once a smart contract is deployed onto a blockchain, it can store an arbitrary state and execute arbitrary computations or call other contracts on the blockchain.

CHAPTER 1   INTRODUCTION

Each smart contract has an address associated with it, which acts as an entry point to the contract, much similar to a URL address for a REST API function. End clients interact with a smart contract by sending transactions using its address via some sort of a client library – a popular choice is ethers.js.

Once deployed, a smart contract cannot be modified. New versions of the contract can be deployed to a different address though.

It is rather popular for the creator of a smart contract to mint a new crypto token, that is, create it out of thin air, which is then used as representation of value on some blockchain network. However, smart contracts may implement other functionalities such as automatic and transparent vote counting, hosting auctions, games, and safely purchasing goods remotely.

The practical applications of smart contracts are outside of the scope of this book.

Consensus Mechanisms

The consensus engine is one of the most important components of a blockchain network, and there are many mechanisms which are currently being developed or in use. For example, proof of work, proof of stake, proof of elapsed time, proof of capacity, and proof of location, to name a few. Their properties influence attributes such as who can participate, how easy it is to participate, how much does it cost to maintain the network, what is the incentive scheme, how fast or how slow block time is, how many nodes can the network support, what is the transaction throughput, and above all how secure the blockchain is!

Check out this list of 20+ algorithms for further reference: https://medium.com/hackernoon/consensuspedia-an-encyclopedia-of-29-consensus-algorithms-e9c4b4b7d08f

Proof of Work (PoW)

Participants in a PoW consensus expend computational resources in order to gain opportunity to append new blocks to the blockchain. They need to solve a CPU-intensive cryptographic puzzle and present its solution, a very big number, to other participants which can very easily compute (agree) that the solution is correct. The data portion of each block is used as input to the cryptographic puzzle.

The first miner that finds a correct solution is given the opportunity to append the new block to the blockchain. Because of this, we say that they **mined a block**.

The more CPU resources a miner has, the bigger chance they get in solving the cryptographic puzzles and appending blocks onto the blockchain, thus earning more rewards for their effort.

In PoW networks, block time is relatively slow, and they have high requirements for electricity.

Proof of Stake (PoS)

Participants in a PoS consensus mechanism compete for the opportunity to append blocks proportional to the amount of crypto tokens they have at stake. In general having more tokens invested is presumed to lead to greater chance of being chosen by the algorithm to append blocks to the blockchain and thus yielding a greater return.

PoS networks avoid the high computational costs of PoW networks. There is no real *mining* because there are far less cryptographic computations involved; however, we often commonly refer to validators as miners even in this case.

Staked funds are held as a hostage by the blockchain implementation and may be taken away from the validator as a penalty if they were reported and found to be at fault or malicious. This process is automated with the goal of limiting human participation and promoting healthy behavior on the blockchain network. For example, when a validator node has been offline for an extended period of time, they will be penalized.

The process of applying penalties and taking away existing funds from a participant in a blockchain network is also known as **slashing**.

Proof of Authority (PoA)

Proof of authority is an algorithm that delivers comparatively fast block times through a consensus mechanism based on identity as a stake or reputation at stake. In PoA networks, individuals earn the right to become validators so there is an incentive to retain the position they have gained. PoA consensus can typically be found in private permissionless blockchains.

Summary

In this chapter, I've covered the basics behind what a blockchain is and talked about some of the main components and attributes of a blockchain implementation in order to establish a baseline of understanding. You can also refer to the glossary section anytime you need a reminder.

Next, I will cover the blockchain development frameworks I've used, some practical notes about building an actual blockchain implementation, and what does that mean for us testers.

CHAPTER 2

Blockchain Development Frameworks

Searching the Internet for "blockchain development frameworks" yields multiple results, and it is entirely possible that preferences will have changed by the time you read this book. Actual details will vary, but basic concepts should be similar. In this chapter, I will list the frameworks I've used personally in order to provide more context for the upcoming chapters.

Hyperledger Sawtooth

Hyperledger Sawtooth is a blockchain development framework by Hyperledger and the Linux Foundation with contributions by IBM, Intel, and others. It is a framework with modular architecture which separates the core system from the application domain, so developers can specify the business rules for applications without needing to know the underlying design of the entire system. Sawtooth supports a variety of consensus algorithms.

CHAPTER 2   BLOCKCHAIN DEVELOPMENT FRAMEWORKS

Originally contributed by Intel, Sawtooth is a blockchain suite designed for versatility and scalability. Transaction business logic is decoupled from the consensus layer into the so-called **Transaction Families** that allow for restricted or unrestrained semantics. Original website: https://wiki.hyperledger.org/display/sawtooth.

Initial versions of Sawtooth were implemented in Python, and later some components were subsequently reimplemented in Rust.

Note   The original Hyperledger Sawtooth repository on GitHub was archived at the request of its maintainers on Feb 1, 2024, during the writing of this book. Ongoing maintenance releases of this code base have since moved under the Splinter community at https://www.splinter.dev/.

Hyperledger Sawtooth was the development framework of choice for the Creditcoin 1.x blockchain which I experienced toward the end of its life cycle.

Substrate

Substrate, https://substrate.io, is a blockchain framework which claims to be the most powerful framework to quickly build customized future-proof blockchains. It is a framework which allows developers to build specialized blockchain applications. Substrate is spearheaded by the Polkadot network and Parity Technologies which are led by Gawin Wood, the first CTO of Ethereum.

Building your own blockchain using Substrate is surprisingly easy, and you can get started in no time just by following their tutorial. See https://docs.substrate.io/tutorials/build-a-blockchain/build-local-blockchain/. The core concept here is composability – your blockchain implementation is composed of multiple components called pallets, which are glued together in a runtime.

Substrate is built with the Rust programming language, while the rest of the Polkadot tooling uses TypeScript – these are usually client libraries and front-end applications.

Creditcoin versions 2.x and later are built using Substrate.

Ethereum

I have not done any development and testing on Ethereum personally but mentioning it here because it is quite popular. Geth seems to be the main Ethereum client implemented in the Go programming language; see https://github.com/ethereum/go-ethereum. Because this implementation is open source, it is entirely possible to fork it and then modify the code in order to create a custom blockchain of your own flavor. This is apparently what the Musicoin chain had done. On the other hand, you are probably far more likely to implement a smart contract deployed on Ethereum main network instead of building a custom chain.

In either case, there are lots of development tools available for Ethereum; see https://ethereum.org/en/developers/docs/frameworks/ if you are interested.

Programming Languages

The programming languages discussed in this book are a colorful mix between Python, C++, and C# .NET during the Creditcoin 1.x timeframe and later primarily Rust and TypeScript for version 2.0 and later.

Rust is a general-purpose programming language that emphasizes performance, type safety, and concurrency. It enforces memory safety without a garbage collector. Rust is a statically typed and strongly typed functional language and is a popular language for systems programming, including distributed systems like blockchain and also the Linux kernel.

Developer Graydon Hoare created Rust as a personal project while working at Mozilla Research in 2006. Mozilla officially sponsored the project in 2009, and since then the language has enjoyed rapid adoption. Here's how the Hello World program looks in Rust.

Listing 2-1. Hello World in Rust

```
fn main() {
    println!("Hello, World!");
}
```

In Rust developers can create user-defined types with the `struct` or `enum` keywords and then attach methods to these types with the `impl` keyword. Rust has been influenced by many other languages and is not entirely object oriented. While you can have user-defined data types with data and methods attached to them, which look like classes, Rust does not have the concept of true OOP inheritance. Instead Rust uses generics, traits, and polymorphism. If traits is unfamiliar to you, you can think about it as an interface definition which needs to be implemented in all data types that are supposed to support that interface.

Using Rust from a testers point of view comes with a few "known issues":

- The compiler is your friend – memory safety pretty much excludes random runtime failures; strong types mean hardly no possibility to mistakenly use a variable in a code block where it wasn't meant to be used (e.g., copy-and-paste issue).

- Nice automated testing facilities built into the language.

- Tests can be executed in parallel.

- Assertions are performed via macros which generate a runtime panic when they fail.

CHAPTER 2   BLOCKCHAIN DEVELOPMENT FRAMEWORKS

- Takes rather long time to compile from scratch so keeping build cache around is important.

- Popular code coverage and static analysis tools may have poor support for Rust because it is still a relatively new language.

- Distinction between "unit" and "integration" test code is relatively small and may not be immediately obvious if you are less experienced with the language.

- There is no syntax for shared setup/teardown as part of the built-in test harness library.

For more information on the Rust language and testing in particular, please see https://doc.rust-lang.org/book/ch11-00-testing.html.

TypeScript is JavaScript with syntax for types. TypeScript is a strongly typed programming language that builds on JavaScript.

Listing 2-2. Hello World in TypeScript

```
const message: string = 'Hello, World!';
console.log(message);
```

The same pros mentioned previously for Rust apply here as well. The TypeScript compiler and linter are tester's best friends and will catch errors for you. A huge bonus is that popular JavaScript testing frameworks have TypeScript bindings and provide more choice for test automation and quite good support from third-party tools and services. Website: https://www.typescriptlang.org/.

In the Substrate/Polkadot ecosystem, the framework of choice is the popular Jest testing framework which I've used quite extensively while testing Creditcoin. If you are coming from a background of test automation for web applications, for instance, you will probably have enough experience to get started very quickly. My personal testing background is rather far away from web and JavaScript, but I got only minor issues getting started.

CHAPTER 2 BLOCKCHAIN DEVELOPMENT FRAMEWORKS

Solidity is a statically typed curly-braces programming language designed for developing smart contracts that run on Ethereum and other EVM compatible chains.

Listing 2-3. Hello World Example in Solidity

```
// compiler version must be greater than or equal to 0.8.24 and less than 0.9.0 pragma solidity ^0.8.24;

contract HelloWorld {
    string public greet = "Hello World!";
}
```

The example above represents a smart contract which stores a specific value, doesn't expose any functions to be called externally, and is included only for illustration purposes. For more information, see https://soliditylang.org/.

While Creditcoin did not start as a smart-contract platform originally, there has always been the need to interface with a smart contract – remember actual loan transfers and repayments in crypto tokens happen on an external blockchain. Later in Creditcoin version 3.0, smart contracts become a first-class citizen.

Testing of smart contracts itself is out of the scope of this book, and I personally don't have experience in this area. It is important to at least be able to read and understand Solidity code for the edge cases where you happen to interact with a smart contract.

How Do You Build a Blockchain Implementation

A blockchain implementation is a complex infrastructure type of software, much like an operating system is or a database management engine is. One could go about implementing all of the respective components and algorithms required in order to have something that looks like and operates like a distributed ledger.

Luckily the majority of the software companies are not operating system or database vendors. Rather these companies are in the business of solving a particular problem for their customers, for example, securely recording loan transactions, by using blockchain technology, thus shifting the focus of blockchain implementations elsewhere.

It seems to me that the majority of practical blockchain-enabled applications today are either built on top of an existing blockchain platform or are built as stand-alone networks using a blockchain development framework or at the very least as a fork of another existing blockchain implementation.

As testers and QA engineers who work with blockchain, we need to have a good understanding of the basic principles but will spend most of our energy testing business domain functionality and specific blockchain components as required by stakeholders. A very small portion of us will actually work on testing the underlying algorithms and complexities involved. Even though I am directly testing the Creditcoin blockchain myself, it is relatively rare that I need to venture deeper into the inner workings of the Substrate framework, especially for the purposes of testing something.

Here's a code snippet of how a blockchain implementation looks like using the Substrate framework (Listing 2-4).

Listing 2-4. Example blockchain runtime implementation in the Substrate framework

```
/// concrete data type definitions
pub type BlockNumber = u32;
pub type Signature = MultiSignature;
pub type AccountId = <Signer as IdentifyAccount>::AccountId;
pub type Signer = <Signature as Verify>::Signer;
pub type AccountIndex = u32;
pub type Balance = u128;
pub type Nonce = u32;
pub type Hash = H256;

/// configuration for various pallets included in the runtime
impl pallet_balances::Config for Runtime {
    type RuntimeEvent = RuntimeEvent;
    type WeightInfo =   pallet_balances::weights::Substrate
                        Weight<Self>;
    type Balance = Balance;
    type DustRemoval = ();
    type ExistentialDeposit = ExistentialDeposit;
    type AccountStore = System;
    type ReserveIdentifier = [u8; 8];
    type RuntimeHoldReason = ();
    type FreezeIdentifier = ();
    type MaxLocks = MaxLocks;
    type MaxReserves = ();
    type MaxHolds = ();
    type MaxFreezes = ();
}
```

CHAPTER 2 BLOCKCHAIN DEVELOPMENT FRAMEWORKS

```
impl pallet_sudo::Config for Runtime {
    type RuntimeEvent = RuntimeEvent;
    type RuntimeCall = RuntimeCall;
    type WeightInfo =    pallet_sudo::weights::Substrate
                         Weight<Self>;
}

impl pallet_evm_chain_id::Config for Runtime {}

/// implement runtime APIs
impl_runtime_apis! {
impl sp_api::Core<Block> for Runtime {
    fn version() -> RuntimeVersion {
        VERSION
    }

    fn execute_block(block: Block) {
        Executive::execute_block(block)
    }

    fn initialize_block(header: &<Block as BlockT>::Header) {
        Executive::initialize_block(header)
    }
}

impl sp_api::Metadata<Block> for Runtime {
    fn metadata() -> OpaqueMetadata {
        OpaqueMetadata::new(Runtime::metadata().into())
    }

    fn metadata_at_version(version: u32) -> Option
    <OpaqueMetadata> {
        Runtime::metadata_at_version(version)
    }
```

```
        fn metadata_versions() -> Vec<u32> {
            Runtime::metadata_versions()
        }
    }
}
```

The full version is available at https://github.com/gluwa/creditcoin3/blob/dev/runtime/src/lib.rs.

Thoughts on Development and Testing

As with any piece of software, how you build stuff has an effect on how you test it.

For example, when working with Hyperledger Sawtooth, it felt like there were too many layers of abstractions, and it was hard for me to wrap my head around all of them. The major drawback in terms of testing is that all components live as separate repositories/docker containers, and it was difficult to test certain functionality in isolation. The obvious choice was to treat everything as one large system and test it from the outside.

In contrast a Substrate-based implementation is more like a monolithic application where everything is bundled up together. I found it much easier to get started and to be productive. The Substrate framework itself also provides facilities for creating a mock runtime in order to test specific components in isolation. This was a huge driver behind being able to build an extensive unit test suite for Creditcoin.

I need to point out that when I talk about a "testing framework," I usually mean the actual facilities and libraries provided within a particular programming language. Since my background is fairly technical and I tend to work with developers directly, there isn't much of *"creating your own testing framework,"* and rather there is a lot of *"just write code, use whatever is already there and get it done"* type of thing, especially when

CHAPTER 2   BLOCKCHAIN DEVELOPMENT FRAMEWORKS

we talk about unit testing. If you the reader is coming from a different background, don't worry. I think it is just important for you to know where I am coming from.

During the initial phase of review for this book, I got a rather interesting feedback from Jeroen Rosink on the topic of using datasets for testing/test automation. And I think we differ here quite a lot. Let me elaborate on this.

In practical terms, I don't keep test data that I get to feed to test scenarios and exercise hundreds of loan transactions in order to find a bug. I am more concerned with the fact whether or not incoming data can be recorded onto the blockchain without crashing and who can record it, for example, a lender or a borrower. Many aspects of input validation are actually handled by the underlying programming languages. For example, I don't need to be explicitly testing that using a negative value isn't allowed when an unsigned integer data type is specified for a given parameter – my compilers are taking care of this and a thorough code review here would suffice.

Another fact to take into consideration is that Creditcoin is a platform, which started to solve a particular business problem and later evolved into a more generic one. On a very high abstraction level, it is just a place where participants in the blockchain can record data onto it. This is not to say there aren't any bugs in Creditcoin, most likely there are; however, when you lean toward building a generic platform, whether that data is 100% accurate and whether or not your software allows the user to shoot themselves in the foot becomes of secondary concern so you plan and prioritize accordingly.

It is also important to note that my practical experience is less of using a test suite exercised against a shared environment, where previous state and existing data can affect its results and/or affect the usability of prepared test data but rather using programming languages to create ephemeral environments on the fly and inject data and model whatever preconditions I need as part of the system under test in order to assert on specific behavior. That is, the majority of testing for Creditcoin happens before anything gets merged and deployed into an existing network. By extension this also negates the need for many testing activities after a new version of the blockchain is deployed. This has probably saved me from having to deal with many practical challenges, but it is certainly something to think about depending on how your organization and you personally approach testing.

Summary

In this chapter, I've introduced the blockchain development frameworks I've used and talked a bit about the differences between them and how that affects testing.

In the next chapter, I will introduce you to what Creditcoin is and how it works which will be the basis for subsequent chapters where I share my testing journey with you.

PART II

The Creditcoin Blockchain: Aims and Objectives

CHAPTER 3

Introducing the Creditcoin Blockchain

One of the main problems that Creditcoin addresses is the fact that millions, and even billions, of people in the developing world do not have access to the traditional banking system – that is, they simply do not have bank accounts. Such individuals cannot use credit as a financial instrument in order to improve their lives because this traditional instrument isn't accessible to them by virtue of them lacking bank accounts. In certain locations, there's probably also a lack of brick-and-mortar infrastructure, for example, bank offices, to enable such access.

Think, for example, of a farmer who is willing to take on debt in order to purchase machinery that will save hours of manual labor and therefore increase productivity. When you do not have access to infrastructure, this simply isn't possible which is where Creditcoin comes in.

What Is Creditcoin

Creditcoin started as a blockchain-agnostic investment protocol which allows participants to lend and borrow any cryptocurrency. On its website, it was also described as "Borderless Financial Platform" which had evolved

CHAPTER 3   INTRODUCING THE CREDITCOIN BLOCKCHAIN

since then. This protocol is detailed in a whitepaper which is published on the https://creditcoin.org website. Its first edition was published in 2017 and has been updated several times since then.

The Creditcoin blockchain is the canonical, open source implementation of the Creditcoin protocol, built and maintained by Gluwa, Inc. It is a blockchain network for investment-related activities, which records loan transactions into a distributed public ledger. This allows representation of real-world assets and facilitates the connection between investors and fundraisers. The records are stored forever on the blockchain, and this data can be used for future credit evaluation by interested parties, for example, traditional lenders.

Versions 1 and 2 mentioned in this book have a more narrow scope toward recording loan-related transactions, while the latest version 3 becomes more generic and evolves into a multichain credit protocol that powers real-world assets with native support of smart contracts. On the https://gluwa.com/ website, this latest iteration is dubbed "Technology that powers global financial inclusion," but I digress.

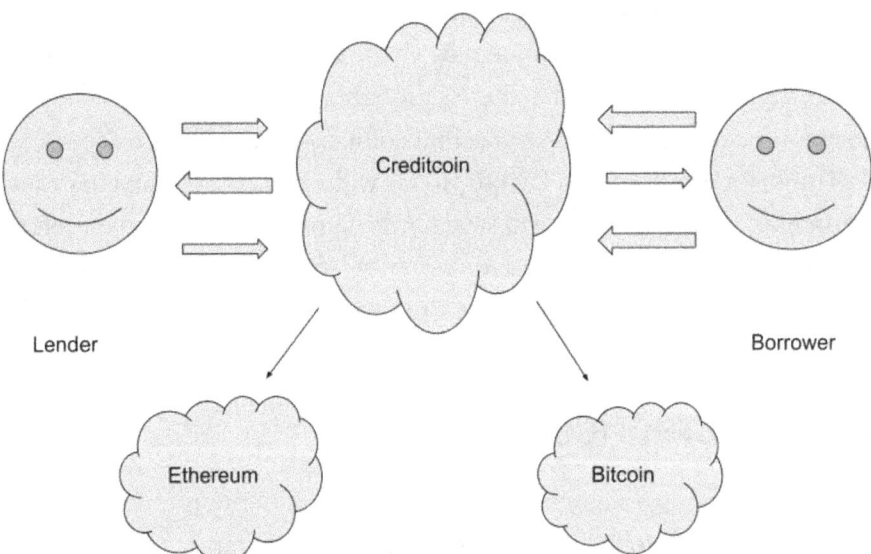

Figure 3-1. Schematic depiction of Creditcoin

44

CHAPTER 3   INTRODUCING THE CREDITCOIN BLOCKCHAIN

Information such as loan terms, repayments, and credit performance are available on the Creditcoin blockchain, facilitating easy and transparent risk assessment and connecting capital from Web3 to real-world credit investment opportunities. The Creditcoin blockchain itself is the necessary infrastructure for enabling the creation of other financial products related to loans, for example, a peer-to-peer lending platform, an investment platform, an exchange, or all of the above combined.

The full schema of the original Creditcoin Loan Cycle is depicted on this page:

`https://docs.creditcoin.org/cc2/faq#how-does-the-creditcoin-network-use-ctc`

Creditcoin is multichain by design as shown on Figure 3-1. Data recorded natively into the Creditcoin chain represents loan terms and agreements and borrowing, lending, and repayment state between participants over time. For example, Alice may record that she is seeking a loan with particular terms, then Bob may record that he's willing to lend under the same terms, and finally a record of their agreement (called a DealOrder) may be recorded. Creditcoin, at least in its original inception, does not support cryptocurrencies, which means that actual asset transfers happen outside of the Creditcoin network. Transfer of assets happens on external blockchain networks and is represented by third-party crypto tokens. For example, if lending in ETH, transactions are recorded on the Ethereum mainnet network. If using a different crypto token to record fiat currency transactions, then we may use other Ethereum-compatible networks such as Goerli or Sepolia. When funding on external blockchain happens, this must be recorded into Creditcoin. The actual record contains a transaction hash valid on the external chain, and the Creditcoin software will go to Ethereum, for example, to inspect and validate the information presented to it. The amount transferred between two participants and their addresses should match their identity and loan terms recorded previously in Creditcoin. Initial Creditcoin implementation in version 1.x came with proof-of-concept code for Bitcoin as well; however, I am not aware if that has ever been used in practice.

CHAPTER 3   INTRODUCING THE CREDITCOIN BLOCKCHAIN

The Creditcoin blockchain validates and records external artifacts such as addresses and transactions on other blockchains onto its own chain and also validates ownership of an address, for example, on Ethereum.

The native crypto token on the Creditcoin blockchain is called CTC. It is used as a utility token to guarantee the economic stability of the blockchain itself. At the time of writing of this book, the CTC token is not used directly for lending.

From a business point of view, the model behind Creditcoin can be described as Infrastructure as a Service. The primary consumer of this blockchain infrastructure will be fintech partners who would like to record transactions onto the blockchain and are willing to access prior credit history and/or gain access to potential new markets and business opportunities that this infrastructure enables. For example, one such partner is Aella in Nigeria. In fact according to the Creditcoin documentation,[1] Aella is the first institutional user of the Creditcoin blockchain, having integrated its operations with Creditcoin in June 2022.

Real humans engage in credit-related activities, for example, the farmer from my example or an investment agent can technically use the blockchain directly; that was even demonstrated in YouTube videos with the Creditcoin 1.x client program; however, I don't think that was meant to be a viable long-term strategy. Such users are far more likely to use a mobile app for their day-to-day interactions, and then this mobile app would communicate with the blockchain infrastructure either directly or via some sort of back-end API layer. In fact Gluwa, Inc. has also been working on such an API layer named Credal[2,3] but I did not have much involvement in this area.

---

[1] https://docs.creditcoin.org/cc2/faq#what-is-the-relationship-between-creditcoin-gluwa-and-aella

[2] https://docs.creditcoin.org/cc2/faq#what-is-credal-what-advantages-does-it-offer

[3] https://credal.io/

All participants in the blockchain will pay transaction fees regardless if they are a physical person exercising just a few transactions or if they are a lending partner who's recording thousands of transactions on the network. The vast majority of the operational expenses, however, are assumed by those running computer nodes which act as the various blockchain nodes; they pay for computing and storage capacity and networking bandwidth most often to a cloud provider.

Impact on Testing Activities

Please note that the timeframe which this book covers coincides with the rapid development and evolution of Creditcoin itself. On one hand, the definition of what Creditcoin is starts to shift toward a more generalized blockchain network, starting with version 3.0. On the other hand, we need to talk about how that impacts testing activities.

As in any fast-paced environment, the actual engineering and testing activities may look very chaotic and are different from what we could find in a more traditional setting or slower moving environment. In particular,

- There isn't much time to formally collect and document in-depth requirements. Often requirement targets themselves will shift while the actual technical implementation is happening.

- Technical details are often unknown and unclear. This isn't uncommon in today's software world due to the presence of multiple layers of abstractions and third-party components used to build software. Perhaps this is a notch higher in the blockchain world due to the inherent complexity in distributed systems.

CHAPTER 3   INTRODUCING THE CREDITCOIN BLOCKCHAIN

- Testing strategy may not be immediately obvious which is a direct consequence of the previous items. Many a time testing would start based on first principles, covering the most obvious positive and negative scenarios and over time be expanded as we gain more knowledge about the system under test. Again not so different from other software testing projects, but maybe contains a bit of a higher risk of missing important testing because the environment itself is higher risk.

- Less choice of available testing tools compared to a more traditional type of application. For example, if I remember correctly when initially looking into client libraries for Substrate, there were two available – one in Python and one in TypeScript. I can find a third one now, written in Rust. While I personally prefer Python, that particular library did not support async functions at the time, and the entire Substrate API is async. So the choice in technology was not really a choice.

Later chapters will document specific scenarios, but it should be noted that there are lots of third-party open source components involved here. In fact, Creditcoin version 3.0 is almost entirely composed of third-party dependencies with very few native components of its own. It is my personal belief that in the case of blockchain, this brings in higher risk compared to web or mobile development.

While for web and mobile you still rely on many third-party components, the organizations behind them are usually not your direct competitors. For example, the Django and Ruby on Rails web frameworks are developed by a large community and are governed by their respective nonprofit foundations for the sole purpose of giving the rest of the IT community better frameworks to create web apps. Another example

CHAPTER 3   INTRODUCING THE CREDITCOIN BLOCKCHAIN

are the React Native and Flutter mobile app frameworks supported by Facebook and Google, respectively. While both Facebook and Google are not independent software vendors, their core business relies on the ability to develop quality applications fast, and they develop a boatload of software, which means they actually have a direct incentive to create good general purpose development frameworks.

Speaking particularly about the Substrate blockchain framework and its ecosystem, their primary developer is Polkadot/Parity Technologies whose core business is running the Polkadot Network blockchain. While they are doing a very good job at providing a general purpose blockchain framework, we have to account for the fact that some components may have higher internal priority than others which is inline with their business goals. In particular I've seen areas in the Polkadot Staking Dashboard code base which have led to issues on the Creditcoin side. That's a situation where the same core technology leads to different severity of known issues and bugs for two different vendors operating in the same domain space. In my opinion, this is a form of a technological risk that needs to be taken into account which exists to a lesser extent in the more traditional web and mobile world.

Due to all of the factors mentioned above, I think the Creditcoin testing strategy can be summarized as **Plan–Build–Test–Discover–Repeat**, or as I like to call it *"Eat, Sleep, Test, Repeat."* That is to say that testing Creditcoin and improving quality has been an iterative process which constantly feeds on itself as new areas and risks are discovered.

It also means that testing a blockchain implementation is tightly coupled with its development, and you can reap the most results by embedding test engineers directly into the development team. I don't think it could have been any other way given all of the constraints already mentioned.

The good news with respect to testing is that although the Creditcoin blockchain is used to record information about real-world financial assets, it does not handle such assets directly. Loan and repayment transfers are

49

initiated by their respective parties on a separate blockchain which means you are not handling transfers directly, only examining and recording information about them. This greatly reduces the associated risk found in any financial services application.

The absolute worst scenario that can happen is complete disruption in service and 100% data loss. This is still a nightmarish scenario from the point of view of business and engineering alike, but it is far less riskier than loss of millions of real financial assets. For the sake of argument, one could engineer around such technical risks by adding redundant service capacity on hot-standby, having good backup and disaster recovery procedures in place, and developing contingency plans in the event the worst comes to pass.

Summary

Now that I've covered the history of Creditcoin and its objectives; let's move onto testing! In the next few chapters, I will talk about my work during the various major versions of the Creditcoin implementation.

PART III

Testing the Creditcoin Blockchain

CHAPTER 4

Creditcoin 1.x

This is the first implementation of Creditcoin using the Hyperledger Sawtooth development framework, initially version 1.0.5 and later switching to version 1.2 of the framework. Creditcoin 1.x is a proof-of-work blockchain. An important side note is that Sawtooth itself was originally written in Python, and in later versions, some of its components were rewritten in Rust. A Sawtooth node represents a collection of multiple components as shown in Figure 4-1.

CHAPTER 4   CREDITCOIN 1.X

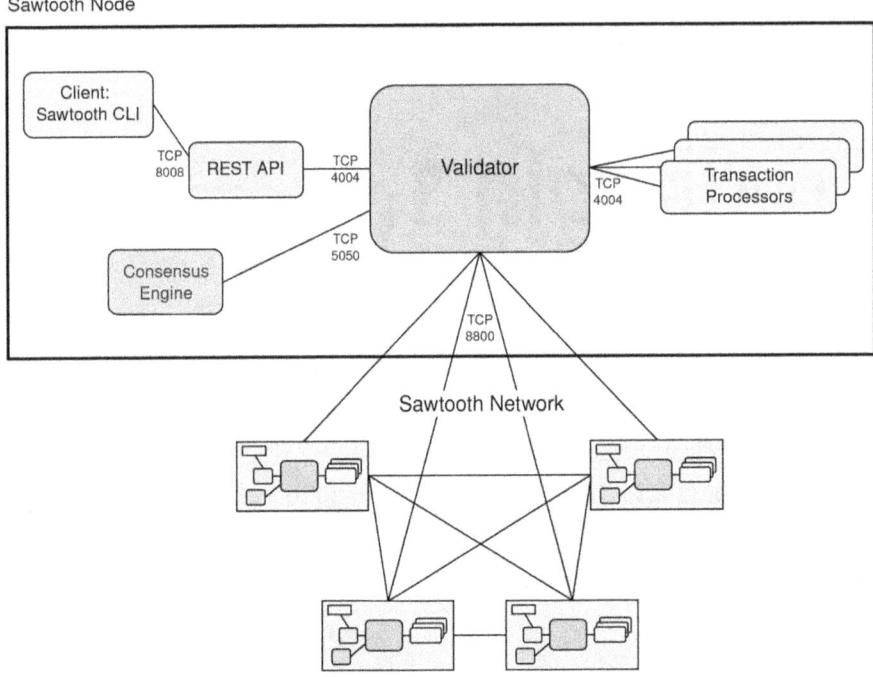

Figure 4-1. *Diagram of multiple Sawtooth nodes participating in a network*
License: Creative Commons Attribution 4.0 International License; see https://github.com/hyperledger/sawtooth-docs/tree/main#license
Source: https://github.com/hyperledger-archives/sawtooth-docs-archive/blob/main/docs/1.2/app_developers_guide/creating_sawtooth_network.md
https://github.com/hyperledger-archives/sawtooth-docs-archive/blob/main/images/1.2/appdev-environment-multi-node.svg

A blockchain implementation with Hyperledger Sawtooth comprises multiple nodes interconnected with one another. In the Sawtooth architecture of Creditcoin, each of the components above is implemented as a stand-alone program and distributed as a container image. A single Creditcoin node is a collection of containers running together, for example, spun up using docker-compose during testing.

Components of Creditcoin 1.x

What follows is a list of the high-level components of Creditcoin 1.x. Always keep in mind that these are completely separate from one another and that they are distributed as independent containers and communicate via each other and with other Creditcoin nodes via several networking protocols! Each of these components may have their own subcomponents!

Client

`ccclient` is a command line program that allows humans to interact with the Creditcoin blockchain by registering their Ethereum addresses, collecting some initial CTC tokens and then participating in the loan cycle as lenders, borrowers, or collectors. This program not only allows the user to send specific transactions to the blockchain but also allows them to perform certain queries. For example, here's how some of these commands look like:

```
list Transfers
list AskOrders
list BidOrders
list Offers

show Balance sighash|0
show Address sighash|0 blockchain address network
show MatchingOrders sighash|0
show CurrentOffers sighash|0
show CreditHistory sighash|0
show NewDeals sighash|0
show Transfer sighash|0 dealOrderId
show CurrentLoans sighash|0
```

```
creditcoin SendFunds amount sighash
creditcoin RegisterAddress blockchain address network
creditcoin RegisterTransfer gain transferId txId
creditcoin AddAskOrder addressId amount interest maturity fee
expiration
creditcoin AddBidOrder addressId amount interest maturity fee
expiration
creditcoin AddOffer askOrderId bidOrderId expiration
creditcoin AddDealOrder offerId expiration

bitcoin RegisterTransfer gain dealOrderId|repaymentOrderId
sourceTxId
ethereum RegisterTransfer gain dealOrderId|repaymentOrderId
erc20 RegisterTransfer gain dealOrderId|repaymentOrderId
```

This application reads configuration from a json file and then communicates with the REST API endpoint of a single node in the Sawtooth network diagram. It can be any node, but usually that's the publicly facing URL for Creditcoin or a node that you may be running yourself. This component is written in C# .NET.

Source code: `https://github.com/gluwa/creditcoin-legacy-client`

Validator

In the Sawtooth framework, the validator component ensures that the same transactions will result in the same state transitions and that the resulting data is the same for all participants in the network. The validator has two major subcomponents that use schedulers to calculate state changes and the resulting Merkle hashes based on transaction processing. These subcomponents are responsible for creating new candidate blocks, completing published blocks and validating proposed blocks to determine if they should be considered for the new chain head. Although the name is the same, please do not confuse this with a validator as defined in the scope of Creditcoin 2 and later.

CHAPTER 4   CREDITCOIN 1.X

While the consensus interface is responsible for determining who can publish a block, whether a published block is valid according to the consensus rules, and which block should become the chain head in the case of a fork, it is the validator component that will publish the blocks.

The validator component in Creditcoin 1.x is based on the `hyperledger/sawtooth-validator:1.0` container image which is implemented in Python. The container image deployed for Creditcoin is a custom build with hotfix patches overwriting the original Python files related to proof of work!

Note that toward the end-of-life of Creditcoin 1.x, there was an attempt to switch to `hyperledger/sawtooth-validator:1.2` which itself is implemented in Rust, with the Creditcoin team contributing a few patches. Due to reasons discussed further in the book, this switch was short-lived.

Another important note is that this component is still part of an older mono-repo, while some of the other components have been converted to stand-alone git repositories! This structure reflects the growth of the engineering team as well as overall reorganization of git repositories that was happening at the same time.

Source code: `https://github.com/gluwa/creditcoin-legacy/tree/dev/PoW`

Consensus

Creditcoin 1.x uses a proof-of-work consensus engine which was developed by the team and connects directly to the Validator component over the internal interconnect protocol in Sawtooth. It is implemented in the Rust programming language. Since the git history doesn't go past the time when I've joined the Creditcoin team, I'm not entirely certain if this consensus implementation is the one which was there from the very beginning or if it replaced another implementation that existed prior.

Source code: `https://github.com/gluwa/creditcoin-legacy-consensus-rust`

CHAPTER 4   CREDITCOIN 1.X

Transaction Processor(s)

In the architecture of the Hyperledger Sawtooth framework, the set of possible transactions are defined by an extensible system called transaction families. Each application defines the custom transaction families for its unique requirements; this is the business logic of the blockchain application. In the case of Creditcoin, that is how we model a loan cycle and record its artifacts onto a blockchain.

The Sawtooth framework allows application developers to write transaction processors in a programming language of their choice. The set of valid transaction families is initially configured inside the genesis block and is kept as an on-chain value which can later be altered. Creditcoin 1.x uses two separate transaction processors which are running independently of each other as separate containers as part of a node.

Settings-tp which started as `hyperledger/sawtooth-settings-tp:1.0` (Python) and later `hyperledger/sawtooth-settings-tp:1.2` (Rust). This transaction processor is responsible for storing on-chain settings like Gateway URL (see below), valid transaction families and their versions, consensus algorithm and its attributes, and others. It acts as a key-value pair stored on the blockchain, and it is also possible to define your own settings to be used by other components.

The **CREDITCOIN** transaction family processor understands what a loan cycle is. Versions evolved from 1.0, 1.1, 1.2 all the way to 1.8. Each transaction sent by a client carries a version number and can be understood by a transaction processor with a compatible version number. In other words, that's how you can upgrade the protocol. The CREDITCOIN family processor will parse the raw transaction payload using the Protocol Buffers data format and also perform some housekeeping tasks like closing expired loan requests before handing off the transaction to the Validator component for writing onto the chain.

Creditcoin transaction processor versions 1.0 through 1.7 have been initially implemented in C++ and used until mid-2021 when I started working on Creditcoin.

Source code: `https://github.com/gluwa/creditcoin-legacy/tree/dev/ccprocessor`

Around the same time, Creditcoin transaction processor was rewritten from scratch using Rust with backward compatible support for families 1.0 through 1.7, and that's what I've mostly used. This new implementation was meant to be deployed as part of the switch to Sawtooth 1.2 mentioned earlier. Note that despite the fact that versioning scheme format looks like compatible SemVer numbers, different versions of the same transaction processor family may be incompatible with one another. This means blockchain operators using an older version may not be able to process transactions coming from newer clients, and they should upgrade. For example, this could be due to a new transaction being added in later versions, which would fail if executed by an older transaction processor.

The last supported transaction family version is 1.8!

Source code: `https://github.com/gluwa/creditcoin-legacy-processor-rust`

REST API

The Sawtooth framework provides a REST API which allows clients and external applications to interact with the blockchain using common HTTP/JSON protocols. It provides a language-neutral interface for submitting transactions and reading blocks. Notably this is useful to query information about blocks during testing using `curl` or libraries for your favorite programming language. All responses are in JSON format.

The REST API is a lightweight layer on top of Sawtooth's internal ZeroMQ/Protobuf communication layer. Clients can bypass the REST API interface entirely and use ZeroMQ/Protobuf to communicate with the blockchain directly if they wish to do so.

The REST API component used in Creditcoin is a fork of `hyperledger/sawtooth-rest-api` with minor cosmetic patches on top. From what I can tell, the usage of a custom container was due to the fact that the original sawtooth-core repository is a mono-repo rather than anything else.

Source code: `https://github.com/gluwa/sawtooth-legacy-core/tree/dev/rest_api`

Gateway

The gateway component facilitates communication with external blockchains in order to validate transfers of crypto tokens. This is the so-called "off-chain worker" component in later versions. That is, it will make sure that when Creditcoin records loan transactions between Lender and Borrower, there are corresponding transfers between the same two parties, for the same amount which are recorded on an external blockchain such as Ethereum.

The Creditcoin gateway listens on a network socket for requests in the form:

`<blockchain> verify <source_address> <destination_address> <proof> <destination_amount> <transaction_id> <networkId or unused>`

The communication protocol between Gateway and the CREDITCOIN transactions processor is ZeroMQ and between Gateway and the blockchain RPC endpoint is target dependent, either using the Nethereum or NBitcoin libraries.

This component is implemented in C# .NET and handles all requests asynchronously and in parallel. Gateway implements the Bitcoin, ERC20, Ethereum, and Ethless plugins with the vision being that other blockchain networks could be supported in the future. As far as I am aware, only Ethereum has been tested and officially supported in production!

Source code: `https://github.com/gluwa/creditcoin-legacy-gateway`

SDKs

Sawtooth-SDK-Rust and Sawtooth-SDK-Cxx are forks of their respective upstream repositories and used in the development of the Creditcoin transaction family processors. They contain a number of patches related to Creditcoin.

Source code: https://github.com/gluwa/sawtooth-legacy-sdk-rust
https://github.com/gluwa/sawtooth-legacy-sdk-cxx

Creditcoin-Shared is C# library used by some of the components written in this programming language, for example, used by the Gateway component.

Source code: https://github.com/gluwa/creditcoin-legacy-shared

Note that after the transition to Creditcoin 2.0, all of the repositories related to 1.x had been renamed to include the **-legacy-** pattern in their names. What we used to call the *processor* during those times is now creditcoin-legacy-processor-rust! In the rest of this book, I will be using the current names when speaking about the various components to minimize the confusion.

Creditcoin-Legacy-Tests

This is the main test suite for the 1.x release series. It is an integration type test suite which sends transactions to the blockchain via an RPC endpoint. It is triggered and executed externally and lives in a separate git repository. The source code repository isn't publicly available unfortunately, so we aren't going to talk much about it in this book.

The majority of the ground work in this repository already existed when I started looking into it, and I've added improvements and new test scenarios but haven't changed the overall architecture of the test suite itself. The same code base was also used as a starting point for

CHAPTER 4 CREDITCOIN 1.X

creating a performance benchmarking tool. This test suite was written predominantly in C# .NET initially using MSTest and later the NUnit testing framework.

Creditcoin-Legacy-Docker-Compose

Docker Compose files for Creditcoin v1.x mainnet. This repository serves as the canonical reference to the various docker images for each component of Creditcoin 1.x and as an example configuration of how to launch necessary components in order to become a participant in the network. It also served as the starting point for creating a configuration used for testing purposes.

   Source code: `https://github.com/gluwa/creditcoin-legacy-docker-compose`

Creditcoin-Legacy-Docker-Compose-Testnet

This is the repository used for testing discussed later. It contains configuration files and references to docker images used for deploying an isolated testing environment.

   Later this repository was also monitored by community members to get information about the latest container versions needed for beta testing the upcoming Creditcoin 1.8 release!

   Source code: `https://github.com/gluwa/creditcoin-legacy-docker-compose-testnet`

Timeline of Creditcoin 1.x

From the public history available on GitHub and Docker Hub, I can piece together the following timeline. It is here mostly for contextual reference.

CHAPTER 4   CREDITCOIN 1.X

1. I started working with the Creditcoin team on June 17, 2021.

2. My first pull request appears to be on July 13, 2021.

3. Creditcoin 1.7.1 was released on July 23, 2021, without participation on my side.

4. Creditcoin 1.8 container images, based on the Sawtooth framework, were released on March 28, 2022, to Docker Hub as the last release for the 1.x network.

Effectively I had been testing the last update in the 1.x family which roughly took around 6 months, so excuse me if information is only partially available. Additional timestamps are provided in further sections.

Testing Creditcoin 1.x

When talking about Creditcoin 1.x and particularly on the topic of testing and generally improving the work of the team so that it can lead to software with higher quality, we must take into account the time period in which this is taking place. In my opinion, it is just inevitable that testing comes together with process and organizational changes.

The period of interest here is roughly the year 2021 during which the team had started using individual public repositories on GitHub for each component. That is also a period during which the team has transitioned to working with a full-time QA engineer, myself, directly embedded into the team.

Timeline of repositories creation:

- Nov 27, 2018: `https://github.com/gluwa/creditcoin-legacy` created.

CHAPTER 4 CREDITCOIN 1.X

- Feb 28, 2019: `https://github.com/gluwa/creditcoin-legacy-docker-compose-testnet` created.
- Jul 29, 2019: `https://github.com/gluwa/creditcoin-legacy-docker-compose` created.
- Apr 14, 2021: `https://github.com/gluwa/sawtooth-legacy-sdk-cxx` first commit in the fork.
- Apr 17, 2021: `https://github.com/gluwa/creditcoin-legacy-shared` created.
- Apr 17, 2021: `https://github.com/gluwa/creditcoin-legacy-client` created.
- May 12, 2021: `https://github.com/gluwa/sawtooth-legacy-core` first commit in the fork.
- May 28, 2021: `https://github.com/gluwa/creditcoin-legacy-processor-rust` created.
- Yours truly joins the team.
- Aug 03, 2021: `https://github.com/gluwa/creditcoin-legacy-consensus-rust` created.
- Sep 21, 2021: `https://github.com/gluwa/sawtooth-legacy-sdk-rust` first commit in the fork.
- Sep 29, 2021: `https://github.com/gluwa/creditcoin-legacy-gateway` created.

Timeline of CI enablement:

- Feb 25, 2020: **creditcoin-legacy-docker-compose-testnet** – CI status for GitHub Pages build, no real testing in this repository.
- Jul 15, 2020: **creditcoin-legacy-docker-compose** – CI status for GitHub Pages build, no testing until after I joined the team.

CHAPTER 4 CREDITCOIN 1.X

- Oct 27, 2020: **sawtooth-legacy-core** – first CI status reported on a commit in the fork, appears to be an Azure pipeline. Configuration file is not in git, and the actual CI job logs are long gone. I assume this was a compile job, and it appears that it hasn't been triggered on every commit judging by commit history on GitHub.

- Apr 14, 2021: **sawtooth-legacy-sdk-cxx** – CI in GitHub; two previous commits in fork. It is running a CMake build inside a docker container.

- Apr 26, 2021: **creditcoin-legacy-shared** – Azure pipeline which is not available anymore, source code not in git, and I assume it was a build/compile job. A bit later in June, there are scanning statuses reported by Snyk, a security scanning service, which are tied to a personal account and later disappear.

- Apr 26, 2021: **creditcoin-legacy-client** – Azure pipeline again, source not in git, pipeline isn't available anymore. I am assuming it was a build job. Later in the year, we can see some statuses reported from Snyk which disappear afterward.

- I joined the team, happy testing!

- Jun 17, 2021: **sawtooth-legacy-core** – first PR with status checks.

- Jun 18, 2021: **creditcoin-legacy** – first CI status.

- Jul 20, 2021: **sawtooth-legacy-core** – first GitHub actions in the fork.

- Jul 20, 2021: **creditcoin-legacy-processor-rust** – first CI status recorded on main branch but not on the default dev branch.

65

CHAPTER 4   CREDITCOIN 1.X

- Aug 09, 2021: **creditcoin-legacy-consensus-rust** – Azure Pipelines.

- Aug 23, 2021: **creditcoin-legacy-docker-compose** – first real testing in CI but never merged.

- Aug 13, 2021: **creditcoin-legacy-consensus-rust** – GitHub Actions.

- Sep 21, 2021: **sawtooth-legacy-sdk-rust** – enable CI in GitHub Actions; 1st commit in fork.

- Sep 29, 2021: **creditcoin-legacy-gateway** – Azure Pipelines and GitHub actions.

State of Testing Before I Joined

As far as we can tell from public GitHub history, two repositories are running GitHub Pages actions, but no real checking on anything related to the software under test itself. Another four repositories are running CI pipelines in Azure DevOps which I speculate that only compile the software without performing much else.

These pipelines in Azure don't seem to have been defined in source code, and their definitions don't seem to have been part of any git repository, so I cannot tell what kind of testing was executed as part of these pipelines. It is also unclear how exactly these Azure CI jobs were triggered and if that has been a reliable event or not since there are some commits and pull requests which don't have statuses reported on them.

Testing Overview

The moment after I joined the Creditcoin team coincided with publishing discrete GitHub repositories for each component. The timeline is after the release of v1.7 and before the release of v1.8.

CHAPTER 4   CREDITCOIN 1.X

At the same time I've been trying to figure out what each component does and what are the testing requirements toward them. I can outline several major areas below.

The private **creditcoin-legacy-tests** test suite and work items related to it which probably consumed the majority of my efforts.

For each individual repository, generally try to figure out where we stand in terms of existing test coverage, and make sure that it has common testing and static analysis tools enabled:

- Enable CI execution for every PR using GitHub Actions. Deprecate older Azure Pipelines which were not kept under git.

- Execute any obvious unit tests (e.g., cargo test), and start collecting coverage metrics where possible to inform further decisions.

- Enable static analysis tools aka linters and code formatters (e.g., cargo check, cargo fmt), and see where we stand. Work on fixing reported issues.

- Start using Dependabot for keeping dependencies up to date.

- Build docker container for the component, and run sanity checks against it because that's how it is supposed to be delivered.

- Experiment with other static analysis tools to see what can be helpful (e.g., SonarCube), and fix some code smells as initial improvements.

For all forks of upstream repositories, try doing the same where possible which wasn't always successful. Keep in mind that for the better part of the first few months, I still don't have a good understanding of how blockchain works in general, much less how the individual components of Creditcoin and their upstream repositories fit together!

67

CHAPTER 4   CREDITCOIN 1.X

On the process side of things, establish a pattern where the test engineer will engage in code review, bug verification, preferably testing directly off of the existing pull request, and moving tickets to DONE **before** anything gets merged! Establish a checklist for code reviews where one of the items is a new unit/integration test being added. Also enable branch protection rules and a minimum of two approvals required before a pull request can be merged. And you may argue that this is not the job of a tester, but I will argue back. If it can improve quality, then it is my job!

In this period I tried becoming more familiar with the Hyperledger Sawtooth framework and the various components of Creditcoin 1.x in order to start adding unit and integration tests written in Rust. Due to priorities, time constraints, and the nature of Sawtooth, that was unsuccessful on my part. I've only managed to add a few obvious unit tests for stand-alone functions here and there but not as much as I wanted. In next chapters, you will see that Creditcoin 2 is the complete opposite of this.

The majority of the focus during this period was on the integration test suite and making use of it for the upcoming v1.7 to v1.8 switchover. The 1.8 transaction family is incompatible with older versions plus there were changes in almost all other components which brought up the need for this migration path to be exercised and tested with more scrutiny.

Due to the fact that a Sawtooth node is represented by multiple individual components, each one executed as an independent container, being able to test directly off of a pull request isn't easy. You do need hardware resources to be able to launch a stand-alone blockchain, and quite often feature changes may be spread across multiple components. This means testing in isolation isn't practical. In reality what I was often doing was to check out all related pull requests, sometimes cherry-pick related commits into a temporary branch; then rebuild docker images for all components and start a local chain using the docker-compose files mentioned earlier. Then due to the fact that the main test suite is an integration type suite with different access control compared to the rest of the components, i.e., not publicly available on GitHub, the most practical way of executing it was to point its configuration to the newly created chain and kick-off all test scenarios by hand. Not impossible to automate given the existing infrastructure but not super practical either.

Although not impossible, collecting coverage metrics across multiple components distributed in several different repositories, written in several different programming languages, using an integration type test suite was not practical either. Because of this, I don't have a good idea how much and how thoroughly the existing test suite was covering the implementation. I've analyzed the source code of the existing test suite, and as far as I can tell it was exercising all transactions from the loan cycle at least once, including both positive and negative scenarios. Was a test scenario missing, or were some scenarios effectively duplicate with one another I simply don't know, and it wasn't obvious which was the case.

Improvement on Tests

I call this section "Improvement on Tests" because I was still very fresh to all of the components in Creditcoin 1.x, and visualizing and implementing the testing strategy was in its infancy during this period of time. Therefore, this section is more of a notable mention of my early contributions to Creditcoin 1.x summarized from GitHub history.

Work on the private **creditcoin-legacy-tests** test suite and related performance benchmarks.

Crude CI enablement for every pull request – unit tests, linter, collect code coverage – initially to become more familiar with the code base, establish a baseline of "test coverage," and find out an area where I can make some progress. This applies for

- creditcoin-legacy-consensus-rust
- creditcoin-legacy-processor-rust
- creditcoin-legacy-shared

Experiment is the right word I believe in adding small unit tests for some of the components written in Rust. Didn't really spend much time on this task, and at the time the entire component architecture and implementation was still hazy to me, so I wasn't very productive anyway.

Enable branch protection rules and require a minimum of two approvals before merge, including my first process improvement – a pull request template with review checklist as shown in Figure 4-2.

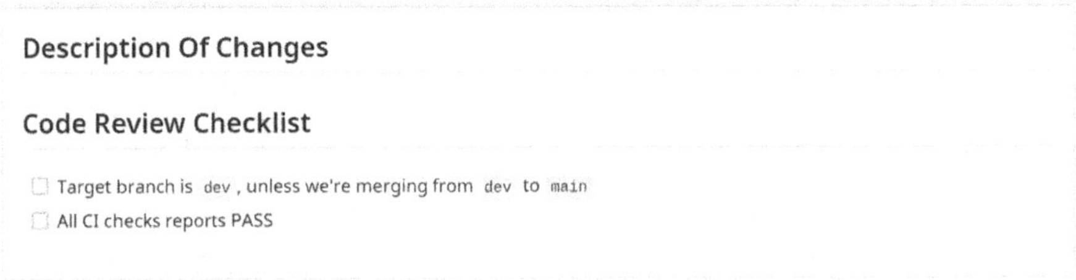

Description Of Changes

Code Review Checklist

☐ Target branch is `dev`, unless we're merging from `dev` to `main`
☐ All CI checks reports PASS

Figure 4-2. *Code Review Checklist*

This checklist later evolved to include more details, but this is one of the earliest versions. While I was writing this book, I saw a similar checklist from a fellow open source project; however, theirs was much better. Each item was a hyperlink to a page providing more details and examples about specific requirements or how to perform a specific task.

Note As testers we should definitely make use of such a format, where checklists link back to documentation and examples, because it is far more productive for everyone working inside the repository!

For forked repositories, **gluwa/sawtooth-legacy-core**; **gluwa/sawtooth-legacy-sdk-rust,** I initially tried enabling GitHub actions with the hope that we can just consume whatever tests they already have. This was short-lived because at the time Hyperledger Sawtooth used Jenkins, not GitHub actions, and I didn't have enough time to work on a full transition nor did I have a desire to deploy and maintain a separate Jenkins instance because of two repositories. Instead I settled for compile, lint, and unit test CI jobs as long as we didn't have to do anything else other than configure the CI pipelines and execute several cargo commands.

I made **creditcoin-legacy-gateway** more robust to malformed messages coming from the outside world, which I discovered while working on an unrelated task. Made it ignore messages which it couldn't parse instead of crashing. As part of exercising the performance benchmarks I was working on, I've also managed to contribute a few optimizations too.

I've made small improvements to `ccclient`; error messages update in several repositories; updated `restart_policy` field in example docker-compose files because I discovered that nodes were running out of memory sometimes and then crashing – mostly small things related to quality of life for the engineering team.

Enable Dependabot on every possible repository, so we can keep up-to-date. For those unaware, Dependabot started as an independent company, later acquired by GitHub, which automatically keeps tabs of your dependencies and opens pull requests whenever a new version is available. This has the added benefit that in case there are incompatibilities between versions your CI jobs will probably fail. It is not 100% guaranteed that if everything in CI is green, then you won't have a problem, but nevertheless Dependabot makes keeping multiple repositories up to date a relatively easy task. It supports a plethora of package management systems including Docker, NuGet, cargo (for Rust), and npm/yarn for Node.js which I was most interested in.

For the C# .NET repositories, primarily **creditcoin-legacy-shared**, I had access to SonarCloud as a static analysis tool which exposed a number of code smells. Then I worked on fixing many of them. Someone may say that this isn't the job of a tester, but I disagree – I am a test engineer and I don't mind fixing code whenever I am capable of doing so.

If we look at a favorite definition of mine:

> *Static analysis is … the analysis of computer software that is performed without actually executing programs… performed on some version of the source code…*
>
> —https://en.wikipedia.org/wiki/Static_program_analysis

Especially references 15, 16, and 17, we are going to see that there is an overlap with the job role of a tester. I am a strong believer in static analysis tools and in fact have used, spoken about, and hosted practical workshops on how to extend or build your own static analysis tools with customized rules which can help you detect certain bugs or possible errors during step #0 of your testing pyramid – before you actually start testing anything else. That is why I tend to use lots of such tools, and in the next chapters, you will see how I've added a few custom ones to prevent possible error conditions for Creditcoin 2.

During the development of Creditcoin 1.8, there was a new transaction added called `RegisterDealOrder`. This is also the reason for the incompatibility with older versions of Creditcoin. This new transaction serves as a convenient entry-point which internally records the same state as several stand-alone transactions. I've worked on new integration and performance tests for RegisterDealOrder as well as actually checking that it results in the same side effects on-chain as produced by the other transactions it was meant to bundle together! A loan is a loan after all, regardless of how many transactions you use to record it into the blockchain – the results must be the same.

Because almost every component of Creditcoin is distributed as a docker image, it was necessary to have CI jobs that constantly build and inspect these containers. Initial testing here focuses on having a `HEALTHCHECK` command in `Dockerfile` and read-only file system inside the container, not the data volume, which are important from an operations point of view. In Creditcoin 2 and 3, this coverage has been extended with the use of extra static analysis tools which detect multiple deviations from industry best practices, but we've also relaxed the requirement for a read-only filesystem.

During the testing campaign, I started publishing a sort of container manifest to let internal and external observers know what we build and what we/they are testing with, see

https://github.com/gluwa/creditcoin-legacy-docker-compose-testnet/pull/7/files. Here's how it looks like.

```
#    This docker-compose file uses the following images below:
#
#    REPOSITORY                      TAG               IMAGE ID       SIZE
#    gluwa/sawtooth-rest-api-priv    testing-2.0-29    7b1d8bd62893   224MB
#    gluwa/creditcoin-validator-priv testing-2.0-29    15887c9ed0ba   390MB
#    gluwa/creditcoin-processor-priv testing-2.0-29    850090b03c6e   2.93GB
#    gluwa/creditcoin-consensus-priv testing-2.0-29    60f3e9b0e887   342MB
#    gluwa/creditcoin-gateway-priv   testing-2.0-29    5a6d120fbd2f   738MB
#
#    Built from:
#
#    Sawtooth-Core (validator/rest-api):
#         - https://github.com/gluwa/Sawtooth-Core/pull/54
#         - https://github.com/gluwa/Sawtooth-Core/pull/55
#         - https://github.com/gluwa/Sawtooth-Core/pull/59
#         - https://github.com/gluwa/Sawtooth-Core/pull/60
#         - https://github.com/gluwa/Sawtooth-Core/pull/61
#         - rebased onto dev@f80dc9d5249dcfe3ee1acb121e44f01c1be0dc67
#    Creditcoin-Processor-Rust:
#         - dev@ac074bcb2899125b2c5ac6197f24d9a4fca86aae
#    Creditcoin-Consensus-Rust:
#         - https://github.com/gluwa/Creditcoin-Consensus-Rust/pull/34
```

CHAPTER 4   CREDITCOIN 1.X

```
#         - https://github.com/gluwa/Creditcoin-Consensus-Rust/pull/19
#         - rebased onto dev@48b19e442cb18300cd43db3f400dce19ecba0a73
#   Creditcoin-Gateway:
#         - dev@e354f2e2a837f7408f5bba21f9a4fa015120b694
```

Testing v1.7 ➤ v1.8 Switchover and Suspected Networking Issues

As part of the existing test suite, I've added extra nodes in order to simulate an older 1.7 node trying to peer with an upgraded 1.8 chain which should not be possible. The actual assertion is as simple as checking the node under test and making sure it did not connect to the rest of the blockchain. A few other scenarios have been added such as keeping track of average block publishing time by introspecting the blockchain under test and sanity checks for so-called house-keeping transactions.

During the testing campaign of Creditcoin 1.8, I primarily worked with a developer to debug a suspected networking issue, possibly multiple issues. Using the existing docker-compose files, we launched a dedicated version of the blockchain spread across multiple cloud providers and geographic regions with slight variations in how network peers are specified – either statically or discovered dynamically. Then using the existing test suite, started sending transactions to this target chain and observed the state of networking. This is the origin of the `creditcoin-legacy-docker-compose-testnet` repository. Later this network was opened to selected community members for even more diversity.

The main items we were looking for were node peering status and presence of forks using the tools at `https://github.com/atodorov/Creditcoin-Tools` since these were the most obvious symptoms of a not completely understood root cause. In practice a blockchain of just 6–10 nodes will not last half a day without some of the nodes losing connectivity between each other, not being able to reconnect and starting their own forks. Sometimes nodes would split into clusters ending into 2 or 3 isolated forks. Manually forcing them to reconnect, for example, by restarting, did not always work, sometimes resulting in forks which couldn't be resolved. Remember that even when validators are disconnected, they still produce blocks because there are transactions which are triggered internally such as timestamps and house-keeping.

This effort went through 41 internal rebuilds, as seen in `https://github.com/gluwa/creditcoin-legacy-docker-compose-testnet/pull/12`, before v1.8 was released. The last time I tested a Creditcoin Sawtooth implementation was on March 15, 2022. `https://github.com/gluwa/creditcoin-legacy-docker-compose-testnet/pull/13`.

The End

Even though we made improvements in multiple areas and upgraded the core Hyperledger Sawtooth components, issues still remained. The Creditcoin documentation contains the following warning:

> *General advisory notes concerning the 1.8 version and release:*
>
> - *Old images cannot be stopped from joining the network and will continue to disturb the network.*
>
> - *Peering issues remain with frequent, long forks occurring.*
>
> - *Nothing stops nodes from starting a network from scratch and attempting to resolve their own chain from very low heights.*

> - *Broken or faulty comms between validator/ consensus can trigger unrecoverable errors in the consensus depending on the missing event/timeout or state in the publishing state machine.*
>
> —The Creditcoin 1.8 change log[1]

A decision was made that we will not continue going in this direction and it would be better to rewrite the blockchain from scratch using a different framework. Substrate was chosen as the replacement technology stack.

Creditcoin v1.8 was published as the last release of the 1.x family, and it was communicated that the next version will be incompatible and community members should gradually move onto the new chain. This final release in the Creditcoin 1.x series is using Hyperledger Sawtooth version 1.2.6.

Summary

What a ride! Join a new team just as they release an upgrade to their flagship product then start testing it only to have everything become end of life in just a few months. I'm certain everyone of us has seen this happen over the years, but I don't recall seeing it happen so quickly ever in my career before.

It is definitely a roller coaster of emotions. On one hand, I felt excited that I was doing something new and challenging; on the other hand, sometimes it was too much to take in and I felt frustrated that I didn't understand most of the inner workings of the software under test and that I wasn't making as much progress as I wanted.

---

[1] https://docs.creditcoin.org/cc2/creditcoin-change-log/version-1.8-2022-03-28

CHAPTER 4 CREDITCOIN 1.X

Maybe it was the technology, maybe it was me, or maybe it was a combination of all of this and more. In the next chapter, you will see how testing becomes a more mature and more structured effort with the introduction of Creditcoin 2.

CHAPTER 5

Creditcoin 2.0

Creditcoin 2.0 is a proof-of-work blockchain implemented using the Substrate framework. It models the same transactions and business logic as the previous 1.8 implementation but was developed independently.

The main objective of Creditcoin 2.0 is protocol compatibility with the previous 1.x version. Here I mean compatibility in terms of all possible transactions listed in the Creditcoin whitepaper being implemented with same or very similar names (allowing for capitalization) and input parameters. What I mean is a logical compatibility with the minimum necessity for changes in the whitepaper and in client side applications. There is no binary compatibility between the 1.8 and 2.0 versions, and they were never meant to be able to operate together with one another.

Creditcoin 2.0 mainnet has been deployed independently of Creditcoin 1.x mainnet, and there is no connection between the two. Because the underlying data structure and technology stack are completely different, interoperability between the two implementations was never a requirement, thus no interoperability testing.

At the time of creating v2.0, there were probably around a million blocks on v1.8 Mainnet, and the only data which were deemed important and needed to be migrated were non-zero CTC balances for all existing accounts which were included in the genesis block for 2.0! In other words, if a user called Jackie had participated in Creditcoin 1.x and had accumulated a balance greater than zero, then she should be able to immediately start using Creditcoin 2.0 with the same account (same public and private keys) and see that her balance is exactly what it was before. This switch is uni-directional.

CHAPTER 5   CREDITCOIN 2.0

The only bits of data that needed to be verified were accounts/balance mappings between the old and the new instance of the blockchain which is relatively easy to do by querying all of the data and comparing it. Not migrating other data, such as existing loan-flow transactions, was a business decision which luckily also removed the need to perform a more comprehensive data consistency testing during the migration process.

For the sake of argument, let's say that preserving chain history was a requirement, but still no need for the two different technological stacks to be connected to one another. In such a scenario, I think that some sort of a replay program would have been a good practical solution:

- Query blocks from 1.x and iterate over the results to introspect each transaction. This is technically possible, and we already knew how to do it because all the necessary technical steps were used as part of the previous `creditcoin-legacy-tests` test suite. The Sawtooth REST API actually exposes this information quite nicely.

- Then repeat each 1.x transaction onto the 2.0 chain using the same input parameters, thus recreating the history. Transaction and block hashes will be different; block numbers will not stay consistent either. Maybe include an old_hash field in each data structure to reference transactions from 1.x for transparency sake.

- For testing purposes, query both chains and "make sure states match" accounting for the difference in data representation between the two! This will be a bit more involved in terms of actual implementation but should be doable.

The same replay program could have been used both as part of testing and migration preparation as well as for the actual migration of production data itself. As we'll see later in this book, preserving chain history became a requirement for the 2.3 release!

The situation where the binary history for the previous tech stack should be preserved, meaning querying blocks and transactions by their existing hashes and having active loan history which essentially spans two different chains, is outside of the scope of this book as I haven't tested anything like that. The easiest way to achieve this that I can imagine is to have both a Substrate node and a Sawtooth node running together plus an additional RPC routing layer which will connect to the respective chain depending on block number. In one version of this imaginary setup, you will have to account for the difference in RPC calls between Hyperledger Sawtooth and Substrate and/or provide a compatibility layer for that as well. Most likely you will have to generate dummy blocks on the new chain to account for the difference in block height.

Another possibility would be to wrap the raw block data from v1.8 into a Substrate block and inject these blocks as part of the launch process for the 2.0 network and provide some sort of compatibility layer as part of the Substrate implementation. Which one would have been easier or more suitable, I cannot say.

Components of Creditcoin 2.0

A blockchain implementation based on the Substrate framework is a monolithic code base which compiles to an executable binary called a node. There are two main parts of the node called the client and the runtime. Application logic, the transactions, and storage items which define what the blockchain does are defined inside the runtime. The client part is responsible for standardized tasks such as peer-to-peer networking, exposing RPCs, consensus, producing blocks, and so on. Unlike the previous version in Creditcoin 2.0, everything is encapsulated into a single running container. The node itself is a multi-threaded application which spawns the various components of the blockchain and executes them in parallel – around 50 or so threads as shown in Listing 5-1.

CHAPTER 5 CREDITCOIN 2.0

Listing 5-1. How a Creditcoin-Node Process Looks from the Operating System Point of View

```
creditcoin3-nod─┬─11*[{creditcoin3-nod}]
                ├─{futures-timer}
                ├─{log-autoflush}
                ├─10*[{offchain-worker}]
                ├─{rocksdb:high}
                ├─5*[{rocksdb:low}]
                └─20*[{tokio-runtime-w}]
```

The Substrate framework utilizes a flexible modular architecture, illustrated in Figure 5-1, and you may extend and/or replace its components relatively easily allowing you to add custom functionality only where needed.

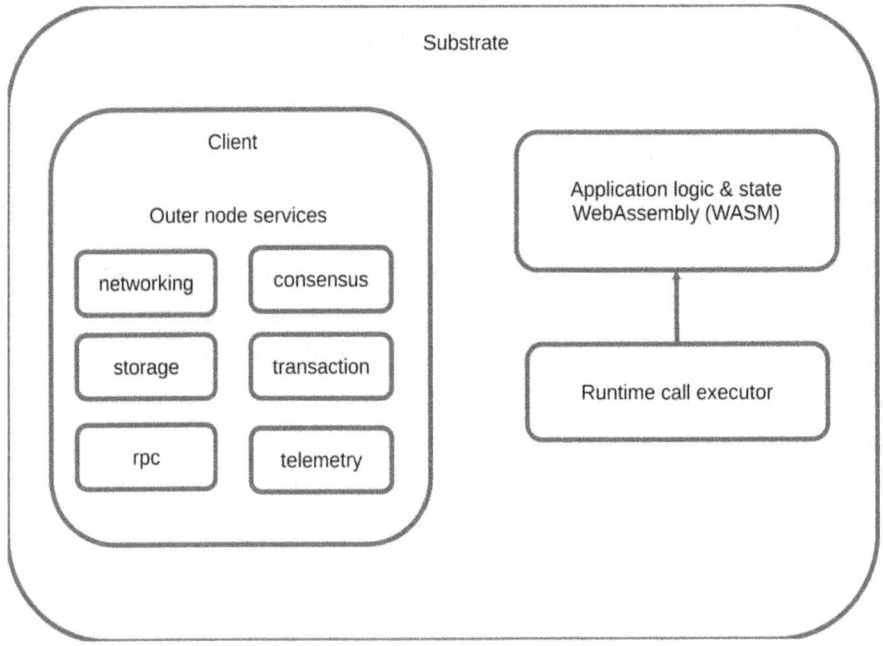

Figure 5-1. *General architecture of the Substrate framework*

Creditcoin 2.0 is implemented in the Rust programming language and shipped as a Docker image, although for testing purposes, most often we compile the code and run it as a stand-alone binary directly.

Source code: https://github.com/gluwa/creditcoin

Extrinsics Pallets

The functions which define what the business logic of the blockchain is are called **extrinsics**. This is what other frameworks call transactions. Inside Creditcoin 2.0, these functions are organized in modules called **pallets**. Creditcoin 2.0 uses some off-the-shelf modules, for example, *sudo* pallet, *system* pallet, *balances*, etc. It also uses custom pallets which are related to the main business logic. See the pallets/ directory inside the source code.

Extrinsic functions are automatically exported via RPC and can be triggered externally using client libraries. This is what the integration test suite and client applications are doing. Extrinsic functions can also be invoked directly when writing unit tests.

Creditcoin Pallet

Defines how a loan cycle is recorded onto the blockchain which is what the Creditcoin whitepaper describes in detail. Provides RPC calls that match the existing Creditcoin 1.x family. The RPC interface and function signature is a logical match but doesn't match the v1.x transactions family verbatim!

This is the main entry point to the blockchain used by integrators and external applications. This is also where the bulk of the testing activities are focused – predominantly functional type testing.

Difficulty Pallet

Difficulty adjustment is an essential component of the PoW consensus algorithm. The so-called difficulty level of the network's cryptographic puzzle ensures that block time stays consistent, prevents centralization and attacks, and maintains the profitability of mining. This pallet is responsible for calculating and adjusting the difficulty on each block. Not used externally and does not expose extrinsics; however, it exposes a few storage items which can be queried externally.

Off-Chain Task Scheduler Pallet

Responsible for executing tasks which need interaction with the outside world, such as validating transfers on another blockchain like Ethereum. Remember that actual loan transfers and repayments happen outside of Creditcoin.

Such interactions are unpredictable and may fail due to variety of reasons. That's why they can't be computed on-chain and need a separate component. The off-chain task scheduler is essentially a queue of pending tasks.

This pallet has read-only access to on-chain storage items in order to facilitate inter-component communication. However, it cannot write to the blockchain directly and needs to call extrinsics to record success or failure for each task that is being processed. Such extrinsic calls are processed in the same way any other regular transaction is.

Rewards Pallet

In Creditcoin 2.0, block miners are rewarded CTC tokens for running nodes on the blockchain. The base reward is 28 CTC tokens per block, which are deposited on-chain when the block is finalized. Recall that in a PoW blockchain, multiple nodes compete for the opportunity to append a block to the blockchain. Whoever manages to do so receives the reward. Whenever starting a Creditcoin 2.0 node, there is the extra option `--mining-key <SS58Address>` which specifies the account address which will be receiving the reward. This pallet is responsible for calculating the actual rewards and depositing them to their respective destination accounts.

Transaction Fees

There is a formula which defines how much fees will be paid for each transaction. Fees can be flat or they can be dynamic. In Creditcoin 2.0, transaction fees are dynamic, with the main component being what's known as weight; see next section.

A business requirement of min 0.01 CTC was established. The actual value and fee formula fluctuates based on chain usage and could drop below the required minimum during periods of inactivity on the chain, especially true when testing on a brand new chain in isolation.

How it works is that we target a block fullness of 25%, so we adjust fees downward if blocks are less than 25% full, and adjust fees upward if blocks are >25% full. It's derived from tokenomics research,[1] and it matches what the Polkadot blockchain uses. Fees can change up to 30% across a 24-hour period.

For more information and technical details, see `https://wiki.polkadot.network/docs/learn-transaction-fees` and `https://github.com/paritytech/substrate/issues/2430`.

---

[1] https://github.com/w3f/research/blob/master/docs/Polkadot/overview/2-token-economics.md

Weights and Benchmarks

Weights represent the computational burden required to execute a specific transaction on the blockchain and are the main component in determining transaction fees. When filling blocks with transactions, there is a maximum weight that can fit into a block. Weights in a Substrate-based chain, such as Creditcoin, are generally denoted as the number of reads and writes on the chain for each extrinsic function. Weights can also vary with hardware configuration.

Benchmarks provide a consistent way to express the amount of time it takes to execute different functions in the runtime and under different conditions. Benchmarks are written by a human developer and then can be used to automatically generate more accurate weights for extrinsic calls!

Usually these benchmarks will be executed on what is designated "reference hardware," and automatically generated weights will be included in the source code. This operation will be repeated on a regular basis, for example, when preparing for a new release.

Reference hardware is whatever you decide given the functional and customer/participants target of the blockchain. For Creditcoin this is a memory optimized `Standard_E4as_v4` virtual machine instance in Azure. Polkadot, the creators of the Substrate framework, recommend more powerful hardware: `n2-standard-8` VM instance on Google Cloud Platform and `c6i.4xlarge` on Amazon Web Services EC2.

Runtime

Inside the `runtime/src/` directory is where all of the components are put together to define what constitutes the Creditcoin node. It's mostly plumbing code which defines concrete data types for all of the pallets involved in the implementation, for example:

```
pub type Moment = u64;

/// Some way of identifying an account on the chain. We
intentionally make it equivalent
/// to the public key of our transaction signing scheme.
pub type AccountId = <Signer as IdentifyAccount>::AccountId;

/// Balance of an account.
pub type Balance = u128;
```

The runtime itself is compiled into WebAssembly (WASM) and can be published on-chain as part of your release process.

When both the natively compiled runtime version and the on-chain runtime version match, a Substrate node will use its native runtime because it is faster. In all other cases, when on-chain and native runtime numbers don't match, the node will use the WASM runtime downloaded from the chain. This is why updating version numbers for a Substrate-based blockchain implementation correctly is important!

This makes the release and upgrade process much easier because miners don't need to upgrade their containers at the same time! It's important to point out that compatibility/interoperability between different native and WASM versions falls within the scope of the Substrate framework itself and has not been tested in detail as part of Creditcoin. I don't recall this ever being a problem because of the preemptive approach taken to version number updates by the team.

Storage Migrations

A good analogy for the actual information stored on-chain is a database for a typical web 2.0 application. Similar to ORM models in Creditcoin 2.0, we have storage items which are data types defining what gets written on-chain, for example, a map between accounts and balances or a map between lenders and borrowers! On the blockchain, this is all in binary format, SCALE, encoded in our implementation.

As business logic and source code changes, we need to perform operations that would transform the binary data from its older format into the desired current format. This is what the migrations component is responsible for, and it behaves similar to database migrations in traditional ORM frameworks.

Migrations are triggered via internal hooks upon upgrade of the WASM runtime and follow an internal numbering scheme. Each individual pallet can have its own migrations, independent of other pallets. In Creditcoin 2.0 outside of the system pallets, only `pallets/creditcoin` contains custom migrations.

Custom RPCs

This component allows you to define and expose additional RPC methods to be used by external applications. These methods can be whatever you decide. In Creditcoin 2.0, it is used to expose some mining-related statistics and a bit of the chain internal information used for monitoring a fleet of running miner nodes.

In the Substrate framework, RPC methods are exposed as JSON-RPC via the HTTP and WebSockets protocols simultaneously.

Telemetry and Custom Metrics

The Substrate framework allows you to automatically expose a telemetry stream to Prometheus – the open source monitoring system and visualize these metrics in Grafana. This component allows you to define your own metrics too which are conveniently available at `<url>:9615/metrics` in plain/text format.

In a couple cases in Creditcoin 2.0, the same data is made available both as Prometheus metrics and via a custom RPC method. Both endpoints call into the same underlying internal functions and serve as wrappers around them.

Another case is also present in Creditcoin 2.0 where custom metrics definitions call into an RPC method to extract information. We call both a custom RPC method and a system defined one, there's no difference between the two.

The fact that similar/same information is exposed as JSON-RPC and Prometheus stream is mainly a convenience decision. You don't need to do both.

Creditcoin-js

Creditcoin-js is a wrapper around the polkadot-js library, which is the primary means of communicating with Substrate-based chains. Creditcoin-js provides some convenience in error handling and cleaner consumer interface. At the time of writing, it is primarily used for integration tests and/or helper scripts.

Creditcoin-squid

This is an indexing and proxy service which ingests the events that happen on the blockchain and records them into a standard RDBMS and then exports a GraphQL API for consumption. It is based on the Subsquid open source project, `https://subsquid.io`, hence the name. The overall architecture of this component is shown in Figure 5-2.

This component is independent of the blockchain and represents an industry-standard means of consuming blockchain-related data by third-party applications. The source code uses the GPL-3.0 open source license; however, at the time of writing, it has not been released publicly!

CHAPTER 5   CREDITCOIN 2.0

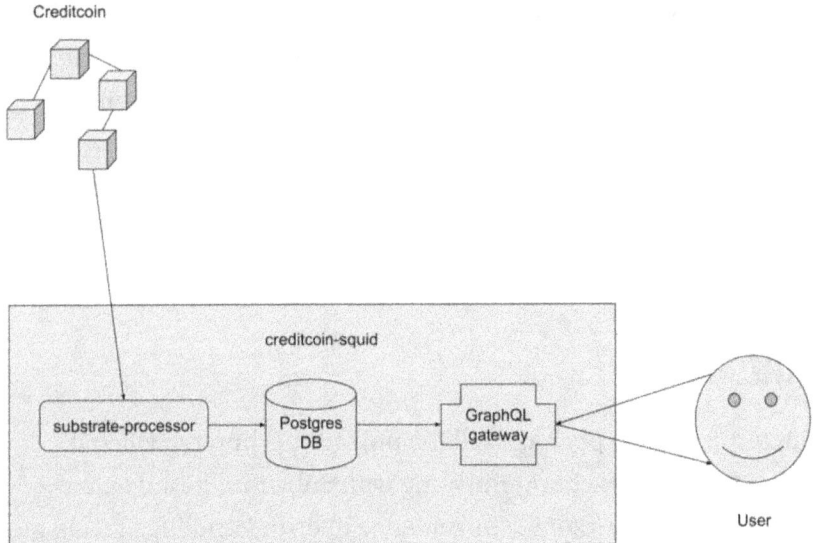

Figure 5-2. *Architecture of creditcoin-squid*

Timeline of Creditcoin 2.0

The lifecycle of Creditcoin 2.0 begins in late November 2021 with a skeleton of the creditcoin pallet built on top of an example code base of a Substrate-based blockchain node. At that I time I was still testing the upcoming 1.8 version, and the 2.0 implementation was still considered an experiment. Later it turned out that it was a viable option to just reimplement everything.

In the following months, all existing extrinsics are implemented, including basic unit testing and cleaning up of the code base and enabling other pallets as additional dependencies are discovered. The implementation is bundled up as a docker image.

The first public release is 2.0.0-beta-2 on Mar 2, 2022, followed by another one, titled Mainnet release: 2.0.0-beta-5 on Mar 23, 2022.[2] Creditcoin 2.0 development continues throughout 2022 and 2023 and eventually becomes Creditcoin 2.3 described further in this book.

Testing of Creditcoin 2.0

Testing for Creditcoin 2.0 started early during its lifecycle and is more organic compared to Creditcoin 1.x. It is also more structured and better defined. The Substrate framework makes it relatively easy to exercise a lot of the functionality via `cargo test` and collect coverage metrics. Everything related to testing Creditcoin 2.0 is automated and is available in its GitHub repository! The CI environment in which these automated tests are executed is GitHub Actions.

Regular CI jobs look like this.

---

[2] https://github.com/gluwa/creditcoin/releases

CHAPTER 5 CREDITCOIN 2.0

- ✅ build-creditcoin-node 41m 3s
- ✅ integration-test-loan-... 12m 27s
- ✅ integration-test-csub-... 16m 28s
- ✅ docker-build 45m 35s
- ✅ sanity-tests 5s
- ❌ danger-will-brick-the-block... 7s
- ✅ cargo audit 6m 7s
- ✅ Rustfmt 21s
- ✅ Clippy 25m 37s
- ✅ check 26m 19s
- ✅ test 50m 36s
- ✅ benchmark 50m 40s
- ✅ Shellcheck 4s

Matrix: javascript-format
- ✅ javascript-format / creditc... 38s
- ✅ javascript-format / integr... 50s
- ✅ javascript-format / scripts... 41s
- ✅ javascript-format / scripts... 55s

Matrix: javascript-lint
- ✅ javascript-lint / creditcoin-js 36s
- ✅ javascript-lint / integratio... 49s
- ✅ javascript-lint / scripts/c... 1m 1s
- ✅ javascript-lint / scripts/js 44s

Matrix: javascript-typecheck
- ✅ javascript-typecheck / cre... 46s
- ✅ javascript-typecheck / int... 42s
- ✅ javascript-typecheck / scri... 44s
- ✅ javascript-typecheck / scri... 41s

while upgrade CI jobs look like this.

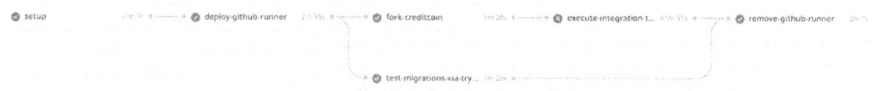

These images have been taken from https://github.com/gluwa/creditcoin/pull/1203/commits, which is toward the end of the original 2.0 lifecycle.

Unit Testing

The Rust programming language comes with its own built-in testing framework, and the entry point for the built-in test runner is the cargo test command! Cargo is the Rust package manager!

Anything that can be exercised easily as a unit test is covered here with the main focus being on extrinsics. For each extrinsic function, we have the positive scenario plus all possible negative scenarios. For the positive case, assert on results in storage and generated events. For the negative scenarios, assert on returned errors with each error condition returning a different error result (differently named type).

```
#[test]
fn close_deal_order_should_error_when_not_signed_by_
borrower() {
    ExtBuilder::default().build_and_execute(|| {
            let test_info = TestInfo::new_defaults();
            let (deal_order_id, deal_order) = test_info.
            create_deal_order();
            let transfer_id = TransferId::new::<Test>(&deal_
            order.blockchain, b"12345678");

            assert_noop!(
                    Creditcoin::close_deal_order(
```

Chapter 5 Creditcoin 2.0

```rust
                        // bogus signature -------v
                        Origin::signed(test_info.lender.
                        account_id),
                        deal_order_id,
                        transfer_id,
                    ),
                    crate::Error::<Test>::NotBorrower
            );
    });
}

#[test]
fn close_deal_order_should_error_when_deal_timestamp_is_in_the_future() {
    ExtBuilder::default().build_and_execute(|| {
            let test_info = TestInfo::new_defaults();
            let (deal_order_id, deal_order) = test_info.create_deal_order();
            let transfer_id = TransferId::new::<Test>(&deal_order.blockchain, b"12345678");

            // simulate deal with a timestamp in the future
            crate::DealOrders::<Test>::mutate(
                    deal_order_id.expiration(),
                    deal_order_id.hash(),
                    |deal_order_storage| {
                            deal_order_storage.as_mut().unwrap().timestamp =
                            Creditcoin::timestamp() + 99999;
                    },
            );
```

```
                assert_noop!(
                        Creditcoin::close_deal_order(
                                Origin::signed(test_info.borrower.
                                account_id),
                                deal_order_id,
                                transfer_id,
                        ),
                        crate::Error::<Test>::MalformedDealOrder
                );
        });
}
```

In this example, ExtBuilder::default().build_and_execute() creates what is known as externalities builder which is a wrapper around a mock runtime in which we can call extrinsic functions and simulate blocks being produced in the blockchain. That allows a lot of the custom chain functionality and error handling to be covered on the unit test level. The execution environment inside ExtBuilder is an in-memory implementation of the on-chain storage. In addition to that, the so-called mock runtime is a partial representation of the real blockchain runtime which may simplify concrete data types and drop unnecessary pallets to make testing easier. For the creditcoin pallet, it looks something like this.

```
// Configure a mock runtime to test the pallet.
frame_support::construct_runtime!(
    pub enum Test where
    Block = Block,
    NodeBlock = Block,
    UncheckedExtrinsic = UncheckedExtrinsic,
    {
            System: frame_system::{Pallet, Call, Config,
            Storage, Event<T>},
```

CHAPTER 5   CREDITCOIN 2.0

```
                Creditcoin: pallet_creditcoin::{Pallet, Call,
                Storage, Event<T>, Config<T>},
                Balances: pallet_balances::{Pallet, Call, Storage,
                Config<T>, Event<T>},
                Timestamp: pallet_timestamp::{Pallet, Call,
                Storage},
                TaskScheduler: pallet_offchain_task_
                scheduler::{Pallet, Storage, Event<T>},
    }
);

parameter_types! {
    pub const BlockHashCount: u64 = 250;
    pub const SS58Prefix: u8 = 42;
    // used in tests, lower values == faster execution
    pub const PendingTxLimit: u32 = 500;
}
```

In this example, the runtime used for unit testing pallets/creditcoin configures only 5 pallets – the target under test and immediate dependencies.

When testing pallets/difficulty, the mocked runtime is even simpler.

```
// Configure a mock runtime to test the pallet.
frame_support::construct_runtime!(
    pub enum Test where
            Block = Block,
            NodeBlock = Block,
            UncheckedExtrinsic = UncheckedExtrinsic,
    {
            System: frame_system::{Pallet, Call, Config,
            Storage, Event<T>},
```

```
            Difficulty: pallet_difficulty::{Pallet, Storage},
            Timestamp: pallet_timestamp::{Pallet, Call,
            Storage},
        }
);
```

For more info on how to get started unit testing in Substrate, see their documentation at https://docs.substrate.io/test/.

Typically the initial unit tests for extrinsics will be created by the developer who implemented said extrinsic function. I would then follow up with more scenarios, corrections, and/or improvements usually around error handling and coverage of corner cases. Sometimes in the same pull request, other times as a separate pull request.

Code coverage metric is the primary source of information whether or not all branches and error conditions of an extrinsic are exercised via unit tests. During the development of Creditcoin 2.0, I've made a deliberate effort to improve this metric and implement as many unit tests as I can. If I remember correctly, the target was 85% coverage, and we came close to 80%.

On some occasions, just to satisfy the metrics, I've added unit tests for helper functions and traits which served to increase coverage percentage but didn't seem to add much value overall. This is purely a speculation though because I hadn't tried to evaluate the effectiveness of this unit test suite with techniques such as mutation test coverage. My rule of thumb was simple: if coverage is missing and it is easy to add a unit test to increase the metric, then do so.

Working on unit tests was also a good opportunity to learn more about how the Substrate framework works and how the Creditcoin implementation is put together. Process wise it strengthened the expectation that QA will constantly perform code review and participate in the development process from an early stage.

CHAPTER 5   CREDITCOIN 2.0

Integration Testing

The integration test suite for Creditcoin 2.0 was born out of several examples of how to interact with the blockchain. I wanted to exercise these examples and make sure that they will still function as we make changes to the implementation – again simple rule of thumb: if it is in git, then it must be constantly exercised and checked!

A crude CI job executing these original examples made us realize that we can refactor the code and make it more usable for consumers. That's why these examples were converted into a TypeScript library called creditcon-js. It is a wrapper around the polkadot/api TypeScript library. Then triggering the examples grew into the integration test suite which became the first consumer of creditcoin-js.

The integration test suite itself is built around the popular Jest testing framework. At the time there wasn't much choice around what languages and testing frameworks to use. On one hand, there was Jest, and the polkadot/api was also used upstream in the Substrate community. On the other hand, there was a Python client library which at the time unfortunately did not support async functions, so it wasn't really a choice.

A simple integration test looks like this.

```
import { Blockchain, Guid } from 'creditcoin-js';
import { KeyringPair } from 'creditcoin-js';
import { createCreditcoinLoanTerms } from 'creditcoin-js/lib/transforms';
import { AddressRegistered } from 'creditcoin-js/lib/extrinsics/register-address';
import { signAccountId } from 'creditcoin-js/lib/utils';
import { creditcoinApi } from 'creditcoin-js';
import { CreditcoinApi } from 'creditcoin-js/lib/types';
import { testData, tryRegisterAddress } from 'creditcoin-js/lib/testUtils';
```

```
import { extractFee } from '../utils';

describe('AddAskOrder', (): void => {
let ccApi: CreditcoinApi;
let lender: KeyringPair;
let lenderRegAddr: AddressRegistered;
let askGuid: Guid;

const { blockchain, expirationBlock, loanTerms, createWallet,
keyring } = testData(
    (global as any).CREDITCOIN_ETHEREUM_CHAIN as Blockchain,
    (global as any).CREDITCOIN_CREATE_WALLET,
);

beforeAll(async () => {
    ccApi = await creditcoinApi((global as any).CREDITCOIN_
    API_URL);
    lender = (global as any).CREDITCOIN_CREATE_SIGNER(keyring,
    'lender');
});

afterAll(async () => {
    await ccApi.api.disconnect();
});

beforeEach(async () => {
    const lenderWallet = createWallet('lender');

    lenderRegAddr = await tryRegisterAddress(
        ccApi,
        lenderWallet.address,
        blockchain,
        signAccountId(ccApi.api, lenderWallet, lender.
        address),
```

```
            lender,
            (global as any).CREDITCOIN_REUSE_EXISTING_ADDRESSES,
        );
        askGuid = Guid.newGuid();
    });

    it('fee is min 0.01 CTC', async (): Promise<void> => {
        const { api } = ccApi;
        return new Promise((resolve, reject): void => {
            const unsubscribe = api.tx.creditcoin
                .addAskOrder(
                    lenderRegAddr.itemId,
                    createCreditcoinLoanTerms(api, loanTerms),
                    expirationBlock,
                    askGuid.toString(),
                )
                .signAndSend(lender, { nonce: -1 }, async ({
                dispatchError, events, status }) => {
                    await extractFee(resolve, reject, unsubscribe,
                    api, dispatchError, events, status);
                })
                .catch((error) => reject(error));
        }).then((fee) => {
            expect(fee).toBeGreaterThanOrEqual((global as any).
            CREDITCOIN_MINIMUM_TXN_FEE);
        });
    });
});
});
```

The core focus of this integration test suite is exercising each available extrinsic to make sure it is accessible from the outside. In terms of actual checking, the primary focus is asserting that transaction fees don't drop below 0.01 CTC. In reality this value is configurable via parameters and allows a margin of error since fees aren't fixed and also depend on how much the blockchain is being used.

Custom RPCs, custom metrics, a few notable error conditions, and a full loancycle are also exercised via this integration test suite, and the results are presented in a nice humanly readable format.

```
PASS src/test/collect-coins.test.ts (49.97 s)
  CollectCoins
    request
      ✓ fee is min 0.01 CTC (10 ms)
      ✓ 000 - with mixed up Ethereum addresses should throw
        IncorrectSender error (11797 ms)
      ✓ 001 - end-to-end (15014 ms)
      ✓ should throw TransactionNotFound when txHash not found
        (9984 ms)
    fail
      ✓ fee is min 0.01 CTC (8 ms)
    persist
      ✓ fee is min 0.01 CTC but bypassed by OCW (8 ms)
PASS src/test/register-funding-transfer.test.ts (59.98 s)
  RegisterFundingTransfer
    ✓ fee is min 0.01 CTC (29060 ms)
    ✓ emits a failure event if transfer is invalid (29987 ms)
PASS src/test/close-deal-order.test.ts (70.005 s)
  CloseDealOrder
    ✓ fee is min 0.01 CTC (69127 ms)
```

Many of these integration tests are controlled by configuration variables, Jest uses configuration files, and sometimes even skipped, because we've added the opportunity to execute them against multiple environments, even against production. In mainnet this serves as a sanity test that loan cycle functionality is still working and that transaction fees meet a minimum requirement.

Sanity Testing and Static Analysis

In this category, I classify most of what doesn't fit elsewhere: linters, code formatters, and custom scripts – I like to follow the best practices set by the language and write clean code. Some of the tools I've used for testing Creditcoin are ShellCheck, cargo fmt, Clippy, eslint, and prettier.

In certain cases, static analysis tools can detect patterns which may be known to cause bugs, so I make sure to create customized tools to check for such patterns in the source code. In some language ecosystems that effort has taken the form of linter plugins, while in the case of Creditcoin these are mostly stand-alone bash scripts. These scripts will inspect the source code, for example, using grep, and alert us about common mistakes which may lead to errors. For example:

- Remember that there are native and on-chain runtimes and which one is used is dependent on the runtime version number? Now imagine the situation where runtime behavior changes but the version number doesn't – this can lead to nodes running code that has different versions. There are a number of situations where the version number needs to be increased so this script takes a preemptive approach and requires version number bump based on a simplified heuristic. Sometimes this version number increase is not strictly necessary but better safe than sorry. It also fits well with the rest of the development process.

CHAPTER 5   CREDITCOIN 2.0

- The order in which extrinsic functions are defined inside their pallets source code directly translates to their internal index in the chain metadata. These indices translate directly to error messages visible to the end user, as resolved by the polkadot-js API library, so we need to make sure that extrinsics order did not change. The bash script is a wrapper around the `polkadot-js-metadata-cmp` tool.

- In order for transaction fees to be accurate, each extrinsic needs an associated weight which is generated by an associated benchmark function. So make sure that all in-house defined pallets have benchmarks, and these benchmarks are hooked into CI for automatic weight generation. Also make sure extrinsic name, benchmark function, and weight function names match to avoid copy-paste errors as much as possible.

- We want to keep up-to-date dependencies and use various security-related tools which generally operate on scanning package versions and matching against popular third-party package repositories. Therefore, using libraries from git repositories, instead of packages, is not prefered. For Rust, prefer package repository crates.io!

- Some of these static analysis scripts are asserting against internal development standards – for example, using or not a particular function or macro. This is for a better quality of life for the blockchain engineering team which usually can be translated to some sort of quality gain for the software itself.

On the sanity spectrum, we are building a docker container and making sure that when started it doesn't crash and that a few common operations can take place – for example, synchronize with an existing live chain; make sure that containers expose a /health endpoint to be used by DevOps for monitoring a running cluster, etc. The container target itself isn't tested 100% explicitly because most of that is the creditcoin-node binary which is tested as part of other test jobs.

Testing with Bots

A number of automatic operations take place during development of Creditcoin 2.0. I call them "testing with bots," but strictly speaking most of these are related to the development process. In any case having them automated has its benefits:

- Menial tasks require less human involvement.
- They happen on a regular basis.
- Pull requests will be opened automatically which in turns kicks off the entire CI/CD pipeline.
- Pull requests will be reviewed and merged as any other pull request,

Dependabot

Automatic upgrades of third-party dependencies are an integral part of Creditcoin 2.0 and future versions and something I've personally been using for a number of years now. This service runs on a schedule and opens pull requests whenever a new version of a dependency library is available. The majority of these are related to creditcoin-js and integration-tests as they are written in TypeScript and receive updates much more frequently. However, even on the Rust side of things, we want to keep as up-to-date as possible. This reduces maintenance burden over the long run, lets you know whether the software under test is still compatible with newer libraries or not, and contributes a tiny bit to improved overall security of your software. If CI jobs are passing, then merge the updated version, usually with only the QA engineer providing review.

A notable exception here is the Substrate framework itself, which is consumed via a git repository. The various components of the Substrate framework are rarely published via crates.io, the Rust package repository, and require manual upgrades. That process isn't automated in Creditcoin 2.0. Technically speaking, it is relatively easy to create your own bot that would propose upgrades for newer versions of the Substrate framework, even when consumed via a git fork. It is my impression that Substrate is still actively changing quite frequently which would require manual work to inspect and assess any incompatibilities so probably not much benefit to be gained by automating this process.

Pre-commit CI

A popular service with Python developers which can modify the source code and create a new commit. Creditcoin 2.0 doesn't use the full capabilities of this service – mainly it uses pre-commit CI to correct missing newline at the end of files, trailing white spaces and some typos. The service itself has not been designed with a Rust or TypeScript code base in mind and the benefit you can get out of it is limited. My main motivation for introducing it – annoying missing newline characters which just make everything look ugly when displaying file contents in a terminal [editor]. Just make the code look nice.

Type Definitions with Gluwa-bot

Any Substrate-based chain serializes its data types and error messages in the SCALE format (binary encoding) and exposes this metadata via RPC. Clients built with the Polkadot JS library can use this to refresh their internal typescript definitions and always keep up-to-date with the blockchain node implementation. This makes type checking JavaScript components work great, which in turn shifts detection of some errors to the static analysis level. Strong types just make a tester's job easier!

Creditcoin 2.0 automatically refreshes type definitions when running test jobs in CI and will automatically commit and push these changes to the current branch of a pull request. To avoid infinite CI loops, the majority of GitHub jobs aren't repeated on the automated commit. To make it clear – all types are updated before any tests are executed in CI, and only if these tests are passing the changes are included into a commit.

Benchmarks and Weights Generation with Gluwa-bot

In Substrate a benchmark is a programmatic way of discovering the computational complexity of an on-chain operation such as an extrinsic. Generally speaking, it is related to the number of storage reads and writes. Benchmark files are written by a human.

Then benchmarks are executed as part of CI to make sure that they compile and that they don't crash. This is the sanity testing portion.

Before a release benchmarks are executed on reference hardware, and the generated weights are committed to the release branch. Because that's different from the dev branch, the same commit is automatically rebased and published as a pull request against the dev branch too. This ensures that everything which gets released also makes it through the dev branch to minimize deviations in the future and the need to resolve conflicts in git, especially during the release process.

Migrations and Upgrade Testing

From the in-house pallets, only `pallet/creditcoin/` actually contains storage migrations. They are named sequentially, v1, v2, v3, etc., and each one of them is exercised via unit test in a mocked environment.

CHAPTER 5 CREDITCOIN 2.0

That is to make sure the migration functions as expected – in other words storage items are actually migrated (think DB migrations in ORM apps). This mocked environment also exercises pre/post migration hooks as an early warning against errors inside of migration functions. Yet some uncertainties remain:

- Have we missed corner cases
- Will the migration work with actual production data

These uncertainties are addressed by two extra test jobs:

1) Simulating the upgrade process and making sure it won't crash
2) Simulating on-chain state and local storage and making sure that storage migrations will be applied without crashing

The same simulations are executed via two different methods:

1. Via `try-runtime`: This is a functionality set made available by the Substrate framework which allows an upgrade and migrations to be simulated in-memory. It will query a production RPC endpoint for the current on-chain state and replicate that locally in memory. Then it will execute the migrations against the local in-memory storage. If nothing fails, we're considering this a success. This can be viewed as a sanity test of runtime upgrades. The detailed upstream documentation is at https://paritytech.github.io/try-runtime-cli/try_runtime/.

2. Fork the chain and upgrade: This method is closer to reality as it consumes the real production data and performs a real runtime upgrade (in isolation).

107

CHAPTER 5   CREDITCOIN 2.0

First we start a creditcoin-node and synchronize with an already existing blockchain – for example, Testnet or Mainnet, depending on which our release target is. Then using a helper tool called creditcoin-fork, https://github.com/gluwa/creditcoin-fork, the current on-chain state will be scraped and recorded into a JSON file. This json file represents a new chain specification, where the genesis block is a replica of the latest on-chain state. That allows you to execute a local chain whose storage items match the production version but still inject development accounts into it and execute it independently. When the newly created local chain is up and running, perform the runtime upgrade which triggers the storage migrations. When that passes, execute the integration test suite against the fork to make sure the fork is still functionally equivalent to the origin.

For upgrade and migrations testing, we're using self-hosted GitHub runners which are deployed on-demand in Azure. This is because the upgrade and migration workflows require lots of memory – 16 GiB at the very least. Block import process is also computationally intensive.

Storage migration hooks are instrumented in two ways in order to facilitate these testing activities:

- A pre and post hook for every migration which allows us to share state before and after the migration for the purposes of assertions. Since storage migrations are executed at runtime, we're making use of the fact that the `assert!` macro in Rust will cause a runtime panic, that is, it will cause the process to crash if the assertion fails. A non-zero exit code will cause the CI job to report a failure.

- A `warn_or_panic!` macro used around if statements whenever an edge case may be present. In a production node, this macro will only produce a warning; however, during testing it will also cause a crash. This behavior is controlled via compiler flags configured explicitly during testing. You can think of this as a last line of defense which you want to see crashing during testing in order to alert you about existing corner cases in production data, but you don't want this to be crashing in production in order not to bring the blockchain down accidentally. The macro does what its name says – either logs a warning or causes a panic.

- A helper static analysis script which fails when migration sources use the `log::warn!` macro directly. This helps ensure that we always use the `warn_or_panic!` macro and don't remove it or circumnavigate it accidentally. Otherwise edge-case branches triggered by actual production data will not fail during testing, and the team may not become aware of that.

In addition to all of this, the creditcoin pallet defines a STORAGE_VERSION constant which must match the number of the last migration. That's also enforced with assertions in every migration as well as with a static analysis script – the number of the last migration file must match the value of the STORAGE_VERSION constant defined in the pallet!

Here is an example of how a migration which moves a storage item between 2 pallets looks like

```
impl<T: Config> Migrate for Migration<T> {

    fn pre_upgrade(&self) -> Vec<u8> {
    let count = Authorities::<T>::iter().count();

    assert!(count != 0, "Authorities not found during migration");
```

```
let old_pallet = TaskScheduler::<T>::name();
let new_pallet = SCHEDULER_PREFIX;

if old_pallet == new_pallet {
log::info!(
target: "runtime::Creditcoin",
"pre-migrate V7, nothing to do.",
);
return vec![];
}

let storage_prefix = Authorities::<T>::storage_prefix();

let new_pallet_prefix = twox_128(new_pallet.as_bytes());
let authorities_prefix = [&new_pallet_prefix,
&twox_128(storage_prefix)[..]].concat();

let new_pallet_prefix_iter = frame_support::storage::KeyPre
fixIterator::new(
authorities_prefix.clone(),
authorities_prefix,
|key| Ok(key.to_vec()),
);

assert!(
new_pallet_prefix_iter.count() == 0,
"Expected new authorities storage to be empty"
);

assert!(<crate::Pallet<T> as GetStorageVersion>::on_chain_storage_version() < 8);

count.to_le_bytes().to_vec()
}
```

```rust
fn migrate(&self) -> Weight {
let count: u32 = Authorities::<T>::iter().count().
saturated_into();

let creditcoin = TaskScheduler::<T>::name();

move_storage_from_pallet(
Authorities::<T>::storage_prefix(),
creditcoin.as_bytes(),
SCHEDULER_PREFIX.as_bytes(),
);

crate::weights::WeightInfo::<T>::migration_v7(count)
}

fn post_upgrade(&self, ctx: Vec<u8>) {
assert_eq!(
StorageVersion::get::<crate::Pallet<T>>(),
7,
"expected storage version to be 7 after migrations complete"
);

let new_pallet = SCHEDULER_PREFIX;
let new_pallet_prefix = twox_128(new_pallet.as_bytes());
let new_pallet_prefix_iter = frame_support::storage::Key
PrefixIterator::new(
new_pallet_prefix.to_vec(),
new_pallet_prefix.to_vec(),
|key| Ok(key.to_vec()),
);

let past_count = usize::from_le_bytes(ctx.try_into().
unwrap());
```

```
    assert_eq!(new_pallet_prefix_iter.count(), past_count);
    }
}
```

The rest of the migrations source code is at https://github.com/gluwa/creditcoin/tree/dev/pallets/creditcoin/src/migrations.

Continuous Testing on Pull Requests, Devnet, Testnet, and Mainnet

Before explaining when testing happens and each individual target, I need to explain the various environments.

>**CI environment**: That's GitHub actions running an isolated blockchain and performing various assertions against it using all of the available test suites and test scripts. Usually in the context of an open pull request, regardless of the target branch!
>
>**Devnet**: That's an instance of the blockchain usually upgraded to the latest available version. The main consumer of this instance is other developer teams working on layered products, for example, mobile and/or front-end applications. The Devnet environment mainly exists for the purposes of developing other applications which communicate with the blockchain and is intended to function as an internal dogfooding environment. This network itself is public but is far less likely to see much participation from external parties compared to Testnet. It is also much more likely that the actual blockchain data in this environment will not be preserved and destroyed over time.

CHAPTER 5   CREDITCOIN 2.0

Testnet: That is a public instance of Creditcoin. It is intended to serve as part of the release process and is updated less frequently than Devnet. It's a soaking place for the upcoming Creditcoin release which is also accessible to the public. Testnet is used both for community testing when necessary, both as a showcase instance of what's coming and also as a playground for loan providers to exercise their own code against (to make sure the latest version doesn't break their own applications). It is possible that this environment may be wiped out, but the expectation is that this will happen only in very rare cases. For all practical purposes, this is considered a production environment. Once an upgrade is made, I explicitly test against this instance to make sure it functions as expected.

Mainnet: That is the production Creditcoin blockchain which is available to the public and loan providers. This is where the canonical information about loan transactions is kept. Once upgraded, I will explicitly perform testing against this environment.

For more documentation around the different environments and their intended usage, please see `https://docs.creditcoin.org/cc2/environments`.

The development and release process for Creditcoin had settled on the following sequence:

1. Each new feature makes it into a pull request which is tested automatically via available test suites as well as manually when necessary going back and forth as needed.

113

2. Every feature pull request is merged into the dev branch. Almost all CI jobs are executed for the dev branch as well. Jobs which automatically create new commits are skipped. They are executed only on pull requests.

3. The WASM runtime from the dev branch gets compiled, and when its version is different from the version on Devnet environment, a runtime upgrade is scheduled automatically.

4. After a while a temporary branch will be created from dev, and a new pull request will be opened against the testnet branch. All available CI jobs execute. The isolated runtime upgrade and migration testing kick off at this point as well. This pull request is the preparation for a new release. Sometimes it may need adjustments because of git conflicts; sometimes it could be a curated selection of commits, not everything currently in dev, etc. Usually we need a mandatory version bump here unless the version has already been updated recently.

5. Merge the pull request from (4) into the testnet branch.

6. Publish a new git tag with the necessary version number. This will build docker container and binary artifacts, upload to Docker Hub, and make a GitHub Release. The suffix is -testnet.

7. Manually upload the WASM runtime to the Testnet environment. Follow up by deploying the newer container version for the client application as well. There is no particular reason why this isn't automated.

8. After a while repeat the process described in (4), and open a pull request bringing code from the testnet branch into the main branch! All available CI jobs, including upgrade and migrations testing, will kick in.

9. Merge to main and git tag, and wait for WASM runtime, docker image, and binary artifacts to be created and attached to a GitHub release. Creating the release itself is fully automated.

10. Manually upgrade Mainnet runtime. Coordinate with DevOps when to upgrade the client containers.

Aside from the unit test, integration test, and various scripts which execute on every one of these pull requests, there are several outlier use cases:

- Runtime upgrade and migration tests will introspect which is their target environment to sync from: either Testnet or Mainnet. The decision is made based on the target branch for a pull request. For example, a pull request against the testnet branch will be testing upgrades and storage migrations against rpc.testnet.creditcoin.network.

- Integration test suite is triggered manually against Testnet or Mainnet **after** a new version has been deployed on each of these environments. Usually that happens immediately after the deployment due to versioning issues with creditcoin-js (used by the test suite). At a later date the easiest way is to checkout the appropriate git commit/git tag, reinstall the necessary Node.js dependencies, and execute the test suite.

Selection of the target environment is performed by passing a configuration file to the Jest test runner, for example, jest --config testnet.config.ts.

- Kicking off integration tests against Testnet and Mainnet is performed by hand. There's no particular reason for this. It can be triggered automatically as well given all the necessary triggers and credentials are safely defined in GitHub CI.

- Testing against any of the Devnet, Testnet, and Mainnet environments requires account credentials and sufficient funds. These are defined via environment variables and are kept secret! Due to security concerns, these accounts don't have sudo permissions! It's also important to mention that these accounts used for testing connect to external blockchains such as Ethereum for the purposes of exercising loan transactions. This also means they operate with real-world crypto tokens which has an impact on the price of testing!

The configuration files used by Jest are TypeScript which look like this:

```
import type { Config } from "@jest/types";
const config: Config.InitialOptions = {
  preset: "ts-jest",
  testEnvironment: "node",
  testTimeout: 240000,
  globalSetup: "./src/devnetSetup.ts",
};

export default config;
```

The globalSetup value is yet another TypeScript file which gives you full flexibility of how you want to control the global state available to Jest and all of the integration test cases. Usually it defines connection URLs, reads actual values from environment variables at runtime, and defines some hard-coded expected values, for example:

```
(global as any).CREDITCOIN_API_URL = 'wss://rpc.devnet.
creditcoin.network/ws';
(global as any).CREDITCOIN_USES_FAST_RUNTIME = false;
(global as any).CREDITCOIN_CREATE_WALLET = createWallet;

(global as any).CREDITCOIN_ETHEREUM_DECREASE_MINING_INTERVAL
= false;
(global as any).CREDITCOIN_ETHEREUM_NAME = 'Sepolia';
const ethereumNodeUrl = process.env.ETHEREUM_NODE_URL;
if (ethereumNodeUrl === undefined) {
    throw new Error('ETHEREUM_NODE_URL environment variable is
    required');
}
(global as any).CREDITCOIN_ETHEREUM_NODE_URL = ethereumNodeUrl;
(global as any).CREDITCOIN_ETHEREUM_USE_HARDHAT_WALLET = false;

(global as any).CREDITCOIN_EXECUTE_SETUP_AUTHORITY = false;
(global as any).CREDITCOIN_NETWORK_LONG_NAME = 'Devnet';
(global as any).CREDITCOIN_NETWORK_SHORT_NAME = 'creditcoin_devnet';
(global as any).CREDITCOIN_REUSE_EXISTING_ADDRESSES = true;

// https://sepolia.etherscan.io/address/0xd2f6CBE058b7233FE5fd
1a790A8D85328e3a5d3D
(global as any).CREDITCOIN_CTC_CONTRACT_ADDRESS =
'0xd2f6CBE058b7233FE5fd1a790A8D85328e3a5d3D';
// we need a new tx hash every time so we call .burn() in
globalSetup()! See ctc-deploy.ts
(global as any).CREDITCOIN_CTC_BURN_TX_HASH = undefined;
```

CHAPTER 5   CREDITCOIN 2.0

Security-Related Testing

There is a sentiment inside the engineering team toward producing a secure implementation of Creditcoin which is loosely defined. Creditcoin 2.0 targets the lowest hanging fruits on the security spectrum. The efforts generally revolve around establishing baseline for security practices, baseline for security-related tools, and baseline for community engagement around security. In no particular order these are

- Keep all dependencies up to date.
- Begin using `rustc` stable instead of nightly.
- Enable popular static analysis tools to figure out which ones are suitable for the Rust ecosystem and Creditcoin, and fix any code smells and issues reported by such tools.
- Enable a low-key security bounty program in order to allow external researchers to find more vulnerabilities and follow up on them.

Tools which I've enabled:

- **Dependabot**: Will update third-party dependencies to latest and greatest and open pull requests. Additionally provides reports inside the GitHub interface about security issues affecting any of your third-party libraries.
- **GitHub's CodeQL**: Static analyzer, supports JavaScript but doesn't support Rust so not very useful.

- **Cargo audit**: a Rust native tool. Reports on CVEs and unmaintained dependencies. We have the report filtered out by first-level dependencies because we have less control over the Substrate framework and the entire dependency stack that it brings. Over time this tool started reporting issues which cannot be fixed unless you upgrade the version of the Substrate framework.

- **MegaLinter's Rust flavor**: A larger collection of linting tools, some of which are relevant to security. It helped us tighten permission for GitHub actions and improve Dockerfile practices. Forced upgrade of some dependencies which had CVEs reported against them.

On the keep-up-to-date front, we don't allow the usage of Rust packages via git repositories because that breaks Dependabot and most other tools – this is enforced by a static analysis script. Notable exception is the Substrate framework itself, which doesn't publish packages on crates.io. Instead we're tracking specific git tags for Substrate. At the time of writing, alerting about newer Substrate versions isn't automated but is fairly straightforward to implement.

Enabling compilation with Rustc stable required several upgrades of Substrate itself, because of the WASM runtime functionality. We had to upgrade one version at a time and resolve the incompatibilities introduced by newer versions of Substrate but finally got there. It is not particularly difficult to do this, but it brings a lot of maintenance burden without clear benefits – anyone who's been trying to keep up-to-date with a popular framework can testify to this – so you probably don't want to be doing this super often if not required.

Testing Creditcoin-squid

Being an indexing proxy, the primary challenge for creditcoin-squid is to maintain data integrity. For testing purposes, it can be summarized as "is the exported data consistent with the blockchain at all times!"

The secondary testing objective is related to the ability to aggregate data from multiple events on the blockchain – do cumulative events function correctly, for example, do we sum up all transaction fees properly!

Initially I looked at property based testing and I was trying to find something like "assert on properties across data records." Eventually I landed onto Slack's Data Consistency Checks framework `https://slack.engineering/data-consistency-checks/` which provided some initial inspiration.

The third big challenge here is that the GraphQL API should expose a stable interface for building layered applications. Thus, any backward incompatible change in the API endpoints has potential to break existing applications and is highly undesirable.

You can use your imagination to figure out creative solutions to these challenges. Unfortunately I cannot share source code or more details here.

How We Found a Bug at Block 1 Million

We did have an environment that was not part of the regular development lifecycle; it was used to conduct performance testing where the network was flooded with thousands of transactions eventually reaching past block 1 million.

This exposed a bug where many records (DealOrders) were set to expire on block 1000000 (hard-coded value from test scripts). The way Creditcoin filters expired entries is by fetching all of them from storage and removing the ones which are not funded and then writes the rest back to storage. This code snippet executes on every block inside a function called on_initialize(). The naive implementation is to read everything from storage, iterate over it, filter items, and write back the rest. That caused memory allocation to grow past a certain boundary and caused a crash.

The temporary solution that the team went for is to keep expired records in storage at the expense of some more disc space being used b/c these are only relevant in the event where you have a loan marketplace which at the time of writing we didn't have so the tradeoff was acceptable. See https://github.com/gluwa/creditcoin/pull/1253 for more details.

The technical background of this bug lies inside the Substrate framework. There is a maximum allocation limit of 32 MB inside the runtime, and Creditcoin was trying to allocate 52 MB; see https://github.com/paritytech/substrate/issues/11132 and https://github.com/paritytech/substrate/pull/11206.

At the time when this appeared, the version of Substrate used to build the production release of Creditcoin was 10 months old so hot-fixing this by cherry-picking commits from upstream may not have been feasible. It could have exposed other risks we weren't aware of so the team didn't go down this path!

These facts just go to show that every piece of testing infrastructure should be treated with the same attention as production infrastructure – monitoring, alerts, and all!

It also goes to show that there may be bugs hidden inside your blockchain implementation that will surface months or even years later, depending on usage volume, and simulating extended usage of the blockchain is important. As fate would have it, Creditcoin 2.3 exhibited a very similar issue.

Other Interesting Facts

As mentioned earlier, transaction fees are not fixed, and they fluctuate depending on blockchain usage. Relatively early in the Creditcoin v2.0 lifecycle, I wanted to exercise this via an integration test and assert that transaction fees increase when the blockchain is "heavily used." Not knowing the precise definition of "heavily used" at the time I went for a straightforward scenario: submit 10 transactions and expect the last fee to be greater than the first one. See https://github.com/gluwa/creditcoin/pull/142/files.

This actually did not work as anticipated because the testing scenario was incorrect. It needs to generate a lot more transactions in order to reach block fullness of 25% and higher over some period of time (blocks), so we can see the internal fee adjustment algorithm kicking into action. The team quickly estimated that we need to be generating thousands of transactions per second. If I'm not mistaken, we were talking in the vicinity of 40000 transactions, but I may be wrong about the number. That's simply not possible with the existing integration test suite.

It may have been possible to use `Promise.all` and the async/parallel nature of Creditcoin RPCs and the TypeScript client library in order to schedule these thousands of transactions. The problem which we then need to resolve is nonce management – that is, the client application needs to generate unique numeric identifiers which would be sent together with each transaction instead of relying on the blockchain to figure this out by itself as it does by default. We didn't have an easy solution at that time, and this was extra work, which was not in scope so the test was abandoned.

Around 6 months later, the team was faced with the challenge of generating loads of transactions again. The context was that we wanted to fill the Testnet environment with lots of records and make it look more similar to Mainnet. That's important, for example, for testing migrations in order to simulate a realistic upgrade scenario and for performance benchmarks. The solution was to create a custom tool called **creditcoin-transaction-producer**, which is capable of producing thousands of parallel transactions and implements proper nonce management.

Another testing area that was explored briefly was enabling the so-called "chaos" pallet as part of the Creditcoin runtime; see https://github.com/gluwa/pallet-chaos/pull/1 and https://github.com/

CHAPTER 5   CREDITCOIN 2.0

gluwa/creditcoin/pull/774. This pallet is mean to inject chaos into an existing runtime and basically try to break your implementation as a means to find edge cases and push the boundaries of your existing code. This was a short-lived attempt because the pallet itself didn't seem very practical in the context of Creditcoin. Upstream Polkadot and other Substrate chains use fuzzing which is more usable in this context, but I didn't try it out.

An interesting issue found was the fact that creditcoin-node didn't always respond to SIGTERM signals and logs were missing so you couldn't tell what was happening. The way that I tested this was with a docker container with artificially imposed resource limits and pressing Ctrl+C on the terminal, https://github.com/gluwa/creditcoin/pull/970. It was discovered that this is a bug in upstream Substrate and was fixed by upgrading to newer versions of the Substrate framework.

Previously I've mentioned how the integration test suite is kicked off manually after deployment on a particular environment. For mainnet, this is using Ethereum mainnet as well; for the rest of the environments, we were initially using the Rinkeby testnet; however, there were sporadic issues with it. After a while we found out that it was going to be deprecated by the Ethereum Foundation on October 5, 2022, so we switched to Goerli testnet. For a short while, we were seeing issues with Gorli as well, in particular high transaction fees. A temporary switch to Sepolia solved that; however, we switched back to Goerli afterward. You can read more about the differences between Goerli and Sepolia here:

https://www.quicknode.com/guides/ethereum-development/getting-started/goerli-vs-sepolia-a-head-to-head-comparison.

A word of caution: note that interactions with external blockchains require additional funds in the form of crypto tokens which means that for Creditcoin Mainnet - Ethereum Mainnet integration the test suite actually burns real ETH coins! That may escalate rather quickly if you aren't careful, especially when dealing with high-value tokens.

CHAPTER 5   CREDITCOIN 2.0

Summary

In this chapter, you can see how testing of Creditcoin was starting to take shape and gradually explore new areas of interest besides the most obvious. It was actually a very pleasant time to work on the blockchain, and I was able to make quite a lot of progress both in testing but also in my own understanding of how the blockchain works.

In the next chapter, I continue telling the story of Creditcoin 2 with another big change – switching the consensus algorithm from proof of work to proof of stake!

CHAPTER 6

Creditcoin 2.3

Creditcoin 2.3 (technical version number), publicly also referred to as Creditcoin 2.0+ (2.0 plus), is the next significant release in the Creditcoin 2.x family. It is a natural successor of v2.0 and builds upon the existing implementation. The most noticeable change is the switch from a proof-of-work to a nominated proof-of-stake (NPoS) consensus algorithm.

Note I will keep using the 2.3 version number in this book in order to make it a bit more explicit when I'm talking about the NPoS variant of Creditcoin 2!

Participants in a proof-of-stake consensus mechanism compete for the opportunity to append blocks to the blockchain proportional to the amount of crypto tokens they have at stake. In general having more tokens staked is presumed to lead to greater chance of being chosen by the algorithm. Nominated proof of stake (NPoS) is a variation of the PoS consensus mechanism which also allows other blockchain participants to vote for validators which act honestly.

Operators running Creditcoin nodes are still known as validators. There is also a new group of participants known as nominators who can vote for validators using their own funds. That is, nominators are saying we trust this validator(s) with our money because they have shown to act in good faith in the past. Remember that in general all of these participants are anonymous.

CHAPTER 6 CREDITCOIN 2.3

Components of Creditcoin 2.3

From an operational point of view, Creditcoin 2.3 introduces several new components to the blockchain, but most everything else stays the same! These components are forks of tools used by the Polkadot blockchain, which is a popular proof-of-stake blockchain and also the creators of the Substrate blockchain framework.

Staking-Related Pallets

This component refers to Substrate's stock pallets which enable staking capabilities such as the ability to stake funds; the ability to vote for validators, penalties, and rewards for PoS participants; and the election mechanism which determines the set of active validators who get to participate in a current era. In Creditcoin 2.3 and later **an era** is defined as 24 hours comprising of **2 sessions** also known as **epochs**.

These pallets are included into the Creditcoin runtime with minor modifications to the pallets themselves. The runtime however defines some values for them, such as expected block time and epoch duration in blocks.

This should not to be confused with the directory `pallets/staking/src` inside the Creditcoin source code. That was part of a former effort to decentralize the off-chain worker component which was later removed. Arguably the naming of this component had been chosen poorly.

Creditcoin-cli

A nominated proof-of-stake blockchain requires a bit more interaction from all participants compared to a proof-of-work chain. While nominators have the Creditcoin Staking Dashboard web application, validators do not have a dedicated web interface. To be fair, there is the Polkadot JS Apps application, also known as the Substrate portal which can be used to configure a validator for any NPoS Substrate compatible blockchain. Instead of using this unbranded generic third-party interface, creditcoin-cli allows users to stake their funds, become validators, and perform a few other maintenance operations.

This is a command line application written in TypeScript which is bundled together inside the docker image. All commands in the cli application talk to the blockchain via a WebSockets RPC endpoint. By default that is ws://127.0.0.1:9944 which is the address on which the creditcoin-node binary accepts RPC connections inside of a running container.

The reason for this bundling together is that some RPC calls are considered unsafe and should not be exposed via the Internet – for example, rotating node session keys. Pretty much everything else is either querying the blockchain or requires the user to sign an extrinsic and can be safely sent over to any available RPC endpoint. The canonical RPC URL for Creditcoin 2 is wss://rpc.mainnet.creditcoin.network/ws, and cli commands can communicate directly with it.

Because Creditcoin is a distributed system, it doesn't really matter which RPC endpoint you will point the cli application to. As long as a transaction is signed and is received by a running node, it will make its way to the underlying blockchain. It is entirely possible that the RPC node receiving the transaction is not the same node which will include said transaction into a block. The only exception here that I can think of is the aforementioned rotate-keys operation which talks to the node directly, doesn't require a signature, and in a way bypasses the blockchain.

Switch_to_pos()

This is a custom extrinsic which lives in a dedicated pallet of a similar name. Its job is to store the block number at which the switch from PoW to PoS happened, raise block difficulty to the maximum in order to prevent any of the existing PoW nodes from producing a block, and initialize the list of validators for the first proof-of-stake session.

CHAPTER 6 CREDITCOIN 2.3

This extrinsic is meant to be executed only once as the last step of migrating to proof-of-stake on production and then never used again. It requires sudo privileges.

This is also the component with the shortest lifetime in the Creditcoin development lifecycle. The majority of it was removed after the switch, leaving only the posSwitch.switchBlockNumber storage item defined.

For the curious, the change happened at block number **715,239** which can be queried directly from the Creditcoin Mainnet; see https://creditcoin.subscan.io/block/715239 and https://polkadot.js.org/apps/?rpc=wss://rpc.mainnet.creditcoin.network/ws#/explorer/query/0x0e754be623e67ba57b51c40a8603342736987b8cdfeacb88819c8457d0a40d93.

You can also query the blockchain storage directly and see when the switch took place as shown in Figure 6-1.

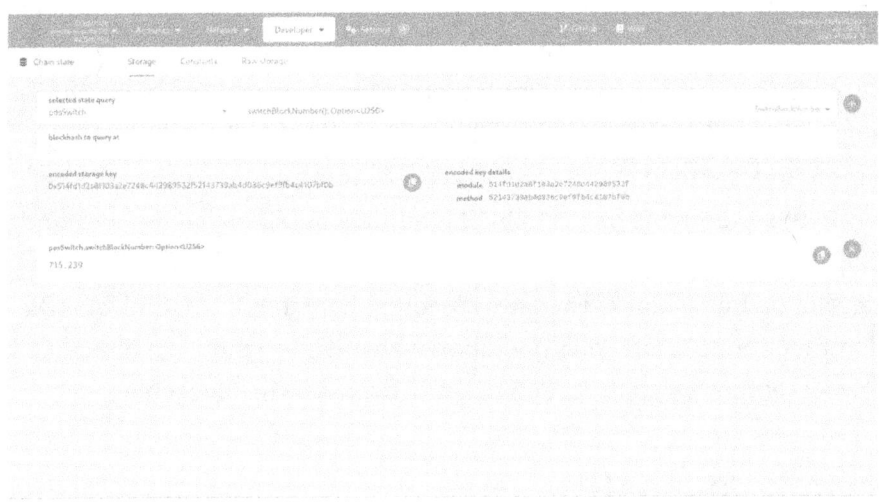

Figure 6-1. *Polkadot/Substrate portal showing at which block number Creditcoin changed to nominated-proof-of-stake consensus*

Block History

Since Creditcoin 2.3 is a natural progression of the existing 2.0 chain, it is important that blocks authored during the proof-of-work period are still available in the chain, and they can still be validated even after switching the consensus algorithm.

The original Substrate implementation assumes proof-of-stake history starts at block zero, and that's hard-coded into multiple locations in the source code. The most straightforward solution was to fork Substrate and modify these hard-coded locations. This is done as part of Gluwa's Substrate fork at https://github.com/gluwa/substrate inside the pos-keep-history branch.

Creditcoin Staking Dashboard

This is a web application which allows nominators to stake their funds and vote for validators. It is a standard React.js application which connects wallet browser extensions, such as SubWallet to the Creditcoin blockchain. The main functionality of Creditcoin Staking Dashboard is staking funds, filtering and voting for validators, and monitoring past performance and rewards.

It is a fork of Polkadot Staking Dashboard with its branding adjusted for Creditcoin, some bug fixes, and simplified functionality. Mainly the functionality around nomination pools was removed because a business decision was made not to include this as part of the migration process. Later in Creditcoin 3.0 nomination pools are introduced back.

Accessible at https://staking.creditcoin.org.

Source code: https://github.com/gluwa/creditcoin-staking-dashboard

Subscan Essentials

Subscan is an API service which monitors dozens of Substrate-based blockchain networks and aggregates information into a SQL database. Subscan Essentials is the open source component which implements this functionality. Most notably the real Subscan software is not actually open source, and an on-premise version is available for a fee. Subscan appears to be using the *open core* development model. From what I could tell, this open source component is not a 1:1 match with the service and has some missing functionality which is to be expected.

This component is used by the Creditcoin Staking Dashboard for the purposes of rendering performance charts, for example, past rewards. It is written in the Go programming language.

Creditcoin 2.3 uses a fork of subscan essentials which adds the missing API endpoints needed by the staking dashboard. The fork also introduces various improvements.

Source: https://github.com/gluwa/subscan-essentials

Creditcoin-squid

This is the same GraphQL indexer as described earlier. There's no substantial new functionality related to proof-of-stake added here so mentioning it just for completeness.

Timeline of Creditcoin 2.3

The timeline for v2.3 stretches roughly from May to September 2023. It is a period of rapid testing and development during which the major components have been fleshed out. This period goes through development, NPoS Testnet announcement plus community engagement, and finally the migration of Creditcoin Mainnet to proof of stake.

Testing of Creditcoin 2.3

The primary goal here is to make sure none of the existing functionalities breaks and that making the switch to nominated proof of stake doesn't bring the existing network down – both in terms of the network staying up; the network keeps producing blocks after the switch and older block history is still accessible!

A secondary testing objective is to make sure that users can assume one of the newly introduced roles, a validator or a nominator, and use the provided applications for these roles without suffering major bugs – this is the new creditcoin-cli and the Creditcoin Staking Dashboard applications.

Any other components may be viewed as lower priority as they have more of a supporting role, rather than being front and center of the user experience!

Unit Tests

New extrinsics such as `switch_to_pos` and a few others added during the Creditcoin 2.3 timeframe received unit tests as per previously established workflow. I've tried to cover all possible scenarios and error conditions and assert on storage changes and emitted events. Nothing out of the ordinary here.

With respect to the NPoS switch, its effects can't really be observed from the unit test level, and trying to model the consensus switch via unit tests doesn't bring practical value because we're using a mocked runtime implementation. This is something which is easier to be observed and checked from the outside.

CHAPTER 6   CREDITCOIN 2.3

Integration Tests

The majority of the preexisting integration test suite stayed the same, and I've added tests for new extrinsics as per the usual workflow. A few tests related to metrics and RPCs had to be removed because they were no longer applicable for proof of stake. For example, because there is no more mining, the node hashrate metric became useless.

Two new items became important before the official switch to proof of stake:

1. Assert that block history is preserved.

2. Incorporate a call to switch_to_pos() as part of the existing upgrade testing procedure.

Asserting on historical block preservation is relatively straightforward:

- Launch a stand-alone blockchain for testing purposes. It still starts as proof of work.

- From outside of the integration test suite, record information about the last proof-of-work block – its hash and block details. Keep this information into a JSON file. Could be done as a setup step inside the test suite itself as well. The reason it happens outside of the test suite is because of the ability to execute this test suite against other chains where the switch had already happened.

- Switch to proof of stake by calling the switch_to_pos() extrinsic.

- Query the blockchain again with the same block hash stored in the JSON file.

- Compare block details – they should be the same as the ones stored in the JSON file!

Simulating the switch as part of the existing upgrade testing is also straightforward:

- Launch a stand-alone blockchain for testing purposes. It still starts as proof of work.
- Synchronize with a target blockchain as before, for example, Testnet.
- Execute the runtimeUpgrade script which uploads the newest WASM runtime blob on chain.
- Either fork and/or disconnect the local node from the target live chain to prevent changes from propagating. We do both in two separate test jobs.
- Call switchToPos() against the locally running node in order to trigger the switch.
- Execute the existing integration test suite against the local node to make sure everything still works. This also includes a check for block history preservation which is baked into the integration test suite.

Tip In the Rust source code, extrinsic functions follow the so-called snake_case naming convention, while in the TypeScript client libraries, the same names are converted to camelCase. Both are the same, but I guess this may lead to some confusion if one is unfamiliar!

CHAPTER 6   CREDITCOIN 2.3

Testing Subscan Essentials

The actual upstream repository of subscan essentials was not in the best state when it comes to testing. History on GitHub showed that CI jobs have been failing for over a year when I last checked, and there is a long list of commits being merged to the main branch with failing CI jobs.

As part of the Creditcoin fork, I've enabled all of the common tools we use on other repositories – MegaLinter, pre-commit CI, Dependabot, CodeQL, etc. Also added golang CI linter as a language specific tool and made sure we have code coverage reporting and CI jobs are executed on each pull request.

Together with this, I've added multiple improvements around setting up required services inside the testing environment – for example, use the existing `docker-compose.yml` setup instead of specifying configuration values in multiple places, using the same golang version as part of CI, and when building docker images, cleaning up Dockerfile and more. Basically make sure that all of the extra tools which are standard practice for Creditcoin are happy and the issues reported by them are resolved.

The good news is that there is an existing test suite written in Go. It is a kind of an API test suite, somewhere between a fully featured integration test suite and a unit test suite as far as I can tell. Its job is to exercise the various API endpoints and assert on their responses.

Developers have tried adding to this existing test suite while working on the new API endpoints; however, we haven't investigated it thoroughly, and it's not really clear to me where we stand in terms of available test coverage (not code coverage) and the quality of this existing test suite. In short I didn't have enough time to dig deeper into this existing code base and find out what was the real state of their test suite.

The confidence in this component can be formulated as such "if it doesn't crash and it doesn't cause Creditcoin Staking Dashboard to produce errors and it seems like Creditcoin Staking Dashboard displays the appropriate rewards graphs then it's probably fine." This was deemed a non mission-critical component hence the formulated acceptance criteria.

Testing Creditcoin Staking Dashboard

The upstream version of this component is at `https://github.com/paritytech/polkadot-staking-dashboard`. If we look more carefully at its test suite from the summer of 2023, we can see that there isn't much in there, not publicly visible at least. CI jobs are executed on every pull request, and they would run linter and build jobs. The only test file I could find is called `graphs.test.ts,` and it exercises a few helper functions. There doesn't seem to be anything else in the form of unit or component testing, nor any sort of visual automated testing with tools such as Selenium or Playwright. Unlike other components from the Polkadot ecosystem, this one doesn't appear to have other test jobs scheduled in a private GitLab CI or Jenkins instance.

Now it is entirely possible that there is internal testing being done on this application and/or automated test suite present as part of another git repository. It's hard for me to believe that there isn't. It is just that I wasn't able to find anything obvious that would be publicly available on GitHub. So not the ideal situation to be in if you are working on a downstream fork but what can you do. It's a risk that you have to accept the moment you fork the git repository and decide to use it.

For the Creditcoin fork, I've gone ahead and enabled all of our standard tools – pre-commit CI, Dependabot, CodeQL, MegaLinter, etc. Some of these tools still report lots of issues against the code base, which were part of the initial state of this component. Not every one of these issues was deemed important enough to be fixed unlike in Creditcoin 3 where all of the reported issues were actually fixed.

Because of the limited timeframe for developing and releasing Creditcoin v2.3, the team agreed on going forward with a simple manual test plan – around 20 test scenarios which cover the most visible aspects of branding and happy path functionality – that is, make sure it funds and nominates validators without any obvious issues or problems. This doesn't mean there are no bugs; of course, there are. It is just that most of them were not critical enough to be a show-stopper. Many bugs were fixed in future downstream releases too.

Keep in mind that this test plan was initially developed following visual clues from the Polkadot Staking Dashboard before any staking functionality was available in Creditcoin and has undergone multiple changes and improvements while being actively executed. It is just one more of these situations where as a tester you have to prepare for the unknown.

In addition every pull request was tested manually – verify that whatever problem is supposed to be fixed was actually fixed and that nothing seems broken as mentioned already above.

On the practical side, this means git check out the pull request, build it locally, and run a local Creditcoin blockchain before being able to reproduce and test these pull requests. This flow has been improved in Creditcoin 3.0.

Testing Creditcoin-cli

Creditcoin-cli is a standard TypeScript application designed to be executed in the terminal, more precisely to be executed inside a running docker container.

There are two main subcomponents which are tested in a fairly straightforward fashion – utility and helper functions are exercised via unit tests, while the actual commands are exercised via an integration test suite in the same way a node operator would trigger these commands. Both test suites are written in TypeScript using the Jest testing framework.

There is a clear separation between these two test suites – unit tests can be executed without any external dependencies, while integration tests require a running creditcoin-node(s) and an Ethereum compatible blockchain (e.g., Hardhat). All of this is running locally in isolation, and the predefined accounts Alice & Bob are used.

In terms of assertions, the integration tests reuse existing helper functions and the blockchain API to assert on expected status. They also assert on command output to stdout!

Due to the fast development pace, creditcoin-cli was initially tested manually simply by using the commands and trying to become a validator inside a PoS chain. I found lots of edge cases, bugs, and small mistakes which have been corrected before the official release. The unit and integration test suites were born out of this experience and at the moment of this writing are still work in progress as most testing efforts are.

An interesting quirk, for example, is that when a new participant wants to join the Creditcoin blockchain, they first need CTC funds in their account. The setup process requires executing the `registerAddress` and `requestCollectCoins` extrinsics. These are meant to allow an external party to prove ownership over an Ethereum wallet and later convert from a G-CRE token on Ethereum into CTC on Creditcoin mainnet.

The trouble here is that both extrinsic calls have transaction fees associated with them, and for a newcomer, there is no way to get started on Creditcoin without external funding. This also presents a problem for testing because we need funded accounts before we can claim any more funds. During isolated testing that's resolved relatively easily by issuing a sudo transaction to update the balance of the testing account because we know the secrets for the sudo account! When testing against Testnet or Mainnet, we need to use already funded accounts, and some steps cannot be executed twice, so you can't really cover all of the testing scenarios.

At the time of writing of this book, this problem still exists and hasn't been resolved. I think it's always been there as part of the interaction flow in Creditcoin but hasn't surfaced earlier because up to this point unassisted external participation has been limited. The easiest way to resolve the problem is probably to drop transaction fees for `registerAddress` and `requestCollectCoins` extrinsics.

The creditcoin-cli test suites automatically collect code coverage metrics and send them to `https://app.codecov.io/gh/gluwa/creditcoin/tree/main/scripts%2Fcc-cli`; however, this metric is not used to inform the development of the test suite. At the time of writing, the focus of the cli integration test suite is to exercise the `wizard` command

and also exercise a full validator cycle simulation as happy-path test scenarios. A few other commands are tested as well, but there wasn't a comprehensive test coverage for all of commands available. Such test coverage was added later, after the initial release of this component.

Testing Gluwa's Substrate Fork

Because of the aforementioned block history preservation functionality, we chose to use a fork of the Substrate framework. A question around staking rewards and penalties made me look more closely into how they were tested upstream. What I found out was not something I endorse as a person who's spent his entire career hacking on open source.

Upstream Substrate executes their testing inside a private GitLab instance. From what I could tell, some of their job definitions use tools and container images which aren't publicly available either. Overall the worst user experience if you are trying to maintain a downstream fork of an open source framework.

Essentially there was no way for the Creditcoin team to know if any of the changes we make aren't breaking Substrate or if any of the newer Substrate versions are incompatible with our own changes before all of that gets merged into a downstream branch and then you try to build Creditcoin against it.

Caution Newer versions of Substrate introduce a significant change to the staking subsystem, for example, consolidating what they call a stash and controller account only into one account which changes signatures for most API/transaction calls related to staking!

After registering a Creditcoin-related group with GitLab, I spent about a week just trying to figure out all of the CI jobs from upstream, finding out where they break, commenting out code or trying some quick patches, and generally exploring the state of it all. It didn't seem to be easy enough and I had the feeling that it would take much longer than anticipated at first, so I needed to implement a contingency testing method for the forked repository.

The team settled on reusing our own private testing infrastructure (on-demand self-hosted GitHub runners) and running `cargo check` and `cargo test`. Even though the hardware resources are deployed in a private environment, their configuration and test results are publicly visible.

We've got static checks via the Rust compiler and the existing unit test suite for Substrate. Note that I call it a "unit test" suite because that's most common when using Rust's built-in testing facilities, but the test suite itself contains hundreds of test scenarios for multiple modules and takes several hours to execute so it probably includes many types of tests. It's yet another piece of third-party code where we don't have all of the details and would have spent too much time if we were to try and figure all of it out.

From my earlier investigation, I had found out that staking rewards and penalties were fairly well exercised via automated test scenarios, and that's what we were interested in anyway. I did try copying the upstream test files into the Creditcoin code base and modifying imports/call paths; however, I quickly realized that this isn't going to work. There were private functions inside the upstream staking pallet which were used as part of existing unit tests, and that meant even more modifications to the fork which was not something I wanted to maintain.

Note that during the Creditcoin 2.3 development effort, there have been new versions of the Substrate framework. We were aware of at least one breaking change that requires more attention downstream. However, a decision was made not to upgrade Substrate during the initial 2.3 development phase in order to minimize the risk of failures and the strain on engineering resources. Because of this, it isn't clear how well the existing downstream CI jobs perform when there are major changes – at the time of this writing, we hadn't yet ventured on this path!

Another important note is that `gluwa/substrate` is following a versioned branch from upstream. If we want to upgrade, then we need to branch off the current code base, rebase against a newer upstream version branch, and see how that goes. This is a manual process which isn't automated at the time of writing of this book. Again more work is necessary to be done here before we can become confident with our testing approach and the ability of the downstream test jobs to detect failures!

Community Testing on PoS Testnet

There is no bug-free software; however, switching the consensus engine of a blockchain is a major event which carries risk to brand damage and community disapproval if not handled correctly. Loss of data, either historical or the ability to produce blocks, is another major risk, which is already covered by the existing test coverage. Here the focus is on the remaining components of the stack.

Internally all components have been ironed out to the point where major bugs and visual flaws do not exist, or they are not immediately obvious to the public after which the proof-of-stake version of Creditcoin was considered good enough to be released as a public beta. A fresh Testnet deployment was made together with the accompanying documentation, Staking Dashboard, Subscan Essentials, and creditcoin-cli components. The first deployment was "PoS Devnet" which was meant for internal consumption by engineering. The community facing environment is called "Creditcoin PoS Testnet."

After this new PoS Testnet environment was created and all of the components deployed, the announcement was made on the Creditcoin website and community channels. Community members were given Testnet CTC tokens and encouraged to participate as both nominators and validators in the network. In other words they were incentivized to exercise the newly introduced software components. This effort was primarily driven by the Marketing team who facilitated collecting feedback from users and compiled a list of bugs and questions from the community that was sent down to the blockchain engineering team.

The purpose of this community testing is mutifaceted and is no different than similar efforts from other software vendors:

1. To generate marketing buzz and community engagement of course.

2. To make sure major components are working as expected, or at least not catastrophically broken and collect bugs and feedback from the actual user base.

3. To make sure that documentation is adequate enough so that users can actually participate and perform expected tasks without hitting technical challenges even when they aren't very experienced in the actual technology. For all we know, some users may be first time participants in a blockchain network. I was one of these users once.

4. To establish a baseline of how many nominators and validators are expected to participate in the network. There are some limitations which I talk about later, and this is a convenient way of collecting realistic data.

5. Allow other engineering teams, both internal and external, to experiment with Creditcoin PoS implementation and adjust their applications if needed. Serve as a staging environment for such teams if you wish.

CHAPTER 6   CREDITCOIN 2.3

A few words about why deploying independently! There are two general options here:

1. Upgrade the existing Creditcoin Testnet blockchain.

    1. Pros

        1. This is what you will actually do on Mainnet; makes sense to keep procedures the same in order to exercise, gain confidence, and potentially uncover issues that have been missed so far.

        2. Allows for real-world testing of the historical block preservation functionality.

        3. The switch is highly visible, and if it goes well, sends positive signals to your community.

    2. Cons

        1. Existing PoW miners may not be aware of when exactly the switch is going to happen which would leave them running without being able to produce a block. Possibly undesirable because they will be expending computing resources and may not be prepared to transition to proof of stake at the same time as you do.

        2. Uncontrolled rapid adoption leading to saturation/overload/corner case bugs – for example, 10000 validators want to join at the same time.

        3. If the switch goes badly, this is also highly visible, and the risk of reputation damage is very high.

3. Contingency

   1. Destroy the broken chain and restore it from a backup. Relatively easy to do in technical terms, may need some coordination with community members but overall very bad publicity if this comes to pass.

2. Deploy a fresh blockchain.

   1. Pros

      1. Completely independent

      2. Allows participants to join as they wish. Existing miners may decide to redirect their hardware resources on their own accord.

      3. Allows you to control who can participate and to limit how many users onboard by controlling the supply of tokens on this new chain as well as control settings how many active validators are permitted, for example, slow growth.

      4. Does not disrupt existing PoW Testnet even if it goes wrong. Still not a good publicity, but the negative effects should be less.

   2. Cons

      1. Does not allow exercising the workflow for performing the switch on Mainnet.

      2. Does not allow testing the historical block preservation feature.

3. Contingency

    1. Destroy the PoS chain and start over from scratch. Still not a good publicity, but the negative effects should be minimal.

Documentation Review

Before the introduction of staking, the existing documentation for version 1.x and 2.0 included a fairly limited amount of user facing instructions. That was the so-called "Creditcoin Mining Node Setup" which basically told the user how to generate a public/private keypair and how to use their public address when starting a Creditcoin container. It has been removed in https://github.com/gluwa/creditcoin/pull/1505.

The new documentation explains the concept of "staking," the differences between proof of work and proof of stake and basic concepts such as Validator Elections, Eras and Sessions, Staking Rewards, and Slashing. A chapter on wallets documents common third-party browser extensions and in-house and third-party command line interfaces. Then there are two new chapters "Nominator Guides" and "Validator Guides" which explain the two main roles in a nominated proof-of-stake blockchain and point the users to the respective application which they can use.

Becoming a validator in a proof-of-stake network is much more involved compared to becoming a miner in a proof-of-work blockchain and also includes multiple independent steps.

Reviewing the documentation, both from QE and other stakeholders, means exactly that – review for typos, grammatical errors, items which don't make sense, terms which aren't clear or not obvious to someone without experience, etc. It was an iterative process with lots of feedback and multiple changes over a short period of time.

The other part of "testing the documentation" is actually following all of the technical steps listed and making sure they are correct; the order is the correct one, and the commands shown will result in the documented outcome, making sure that version numbers, URLs, etc. are also the correct ones.

Some sections of the documentation contain examples for platforms different from Linux, so you need someone to verify that they are actually correct. After a while working with this document, one becomes fairly biased and starts skipping sections from the docs or already anticipates which commands you need to type, so double-checking everything super diligently becomes a chore. This is when you have to bring in other team members, preferably ones who have less experience and/or are unfamiliar with the documentation and the overall "become a validator" workflow so they can spot more edge cases and help improve the documentation.

Documentation URL: `https://docs.creditcoin.org/cc2` (different from the Creditcoin 3.0 docs).

Load and Performance Testing

In the context of nominated proof of stake, the questions around performance of the blockchain became important again. There are multiple items happening at the same time:

- The algorithm selecting validators for the next era is effectively traversing a graph. The bigger the number of validators, the bigger the graph which takes more time to solve. If I remember correctly, Web3 research documents a practical limit around 300 validators, and other Substrate chains like Kusama and Polkadot are already running at this limit. For Creditcoin it's important to find out what is our practical limit.

- There is also a setting which limits the number of nominators per validator. It's unclear to me how this number influences the graph algorithm from the previous item if at all.

- All validators are sending an i-am-online ping throughout the current era; otherwise, they will be penalized.

- The penalty subsystem is monitoring online pings and calculating penalties when necessary, chilling off validator nodes if need be.

- Based on the number of blocks produced by each validator during the current era, the rewards subsystem is calculating rewards for the validator and all of their nominators.

- There are the regular Creditcoin loan-cycle transactions.

The entire blockchain is far more chattier compared to its proof-of-work predecessor.

Looking at all of this for Creditcoin 2.3, we needed to establish a performance baseline and a toolset/methodology of doing "performance testing." Using quotes here because I've merely been scratching the surface in this area, not going deep enough as you'll see.

The first tool in the arsenal is called Zombienet, `https://github.com/paritytech/zombienet`. It uses templates and will launch a stand-alone ephemeral blockchain network. Using the template files, it is possible to configure a different number of nodes and parameters. You may also use the Zombienet DSL language to assert against the spawned network!

CHAPTER 6 CREDITCOIN 2.3

I used Zombienet to launch networks of 100 to 300 validators and adjust Creditcoin settings, to establish a baseline of hardware requirements for testing and a baseline of behavior for the network. The entrypoint for Creditcoin Zombienet is the `zombienet/` directory inside the main git repository.

The next important question was "if we switch to nominated proof of stake, can Creditcoin support a minimum number of loan transactions" or rather "how many loan transactions can it support"? In other words, does the switch to a proof of stake have any impact on blockchain throughput from a business point of view? Initially we looked at https://github.com/paritytech/polkadot-stps which is a generic tool for any Substrate-based chain. Polkadot-STPS sends balance transfers which are virtually guaranteed to exist in every blockchain implementation using the Substrate framework; however, they are fairly lightweight compared to loan cycle transactions so not the best fit.

I didn't go deeper into this rabbit hole because the data that was found out initially answered the most important questions toward the expected blockchain performance in the near to mid-term future. There is also the tool creditcoin-transaction-producer created by another team member whose job is to send hundreds and thousands of transactions and actually answer the questions around throughput.

Security Bounty Program

Security has been and still is an ongoing concern for Creditcoin. And in my personal opinion, we as engineers should always strive to create secure software and be thinking along those lines.

For example, as part of the development of `creditcoin-cli`, I've successfully advocated for removing the ability to directly specify secrets in plain text or display them as such in the terminal. Such functionality poses a security concern because these plain text values may end up in a terminal history file or copy-pasted to a wider audience with command output while trying to report a problem, etc. I've been working in the industry long enough to have firsthand experience of experienced teams leaking their credentials on the Internet via a number of different means. Having your software expose secrets in plain text without a minimum precaution is a sure way for less security-cautious/tech-savvy users to leak their secrets. You are just asking for it!

In creditcoin-cli secrets are either read interactively via a terminal prompt which masks the input characters and doesn't allow the value to be copied, or they need to be specified as environment variables! These values are never stored on disk by the application itself.

Aside from Creditcoin engineers doing internal assessment on the risks from a security point of view and the already mentioned static analysis tools, following best practices, and keeping third-party dependencies up-to-date, the team made some more work on our security bounty program.

It is a low-key bounty program originally hosted at the Hunter.dev platform which had changed focus since then and documents the steps to responsibly disclose security vulnerabilities inside a SECURITY.md file in each repository. The goal is to allow the community to discover any low hanging fruits and for the team to establish a workflow around patching and responding to security vulnerabilities. For testing that means validating the reported entries, most importantly making sure steps to reproduce and issue description are accurate to the point where an engineer can work on them.

The next step in this security journey will be a dedicated security bounty program with high monetary or crypto rewards which is hosted on a higher profile platform dedicated to Web3 security research. At the time of writing, the team is not there yet.

Note that during the writing of this book, the huntr.dev platform itself changed ownership and shifted their focus from a general-purpose security bounty platform into one targeting AI/ML. Thus the original bounty program is no more! Security vulnerabilities can still be disclosed

CHAPTER 6   CREDITCOIN 2.3

via email and/or GitHub's security advisory interface which is accessible to everyone, but isn't specifically targeting professionals in the security research space.

As it happens, I've also worked on crafting a couple of security advisories for Creditcoin that were eventually published under `https://github.com/gluwa/creditcoin/security/advisories`. One more thing for test engineers to add under their toolbelts!

Other Interesting Testing and Some Bugs

As part of v2.3 development, a number of interesting failures happened. They happened on dedicated testing environments and prompted more testing to be added to the existing suite.

Once you switch to nominated proof of stake, you can't change some values inside your blockchain implementation. Most importantly can't change duration of staking epoch – the period for which validators are chosen to produce blocks! Changing this bricks the blockchain so I've added static analysis checks and integration tests to catch this! Which also highlights how important choosing the actual values here is.

Another issue related to upgrade testing infrastructure is how latest releases are discovered based on git tags. The CI jobs expect a certain naming convention, for example, -devnet for upgrades intended for Devnet, -testnet for Testnet, and so on. Remember how the runtime upgrade testing CI jobs introspect the target branch for a pull request in order to figure out which chain to synchronize to? In a similar fashion, they need to know how to find the previous release which is used in several different places as part of those CI jobs. Consistently naming releases is important, and several versions broke the existing convention which negatively affected CI jobs execution for future releases. That's been fixed by bumping the version number and tagging new releases in GitHub with the appropriate names. On the testing side, I've added another static analysis script to actually break the release pipeline in case the naming

149

convention isn't followed. I bet you didn't imagine that naming your git tags is something that would require testing, but when you turn it into a public interface, then it does need to be tested.

When I was working on setting up the load testing tools, briefly I had an issue where `creditcoin-transaction-producer` wasn't working with the latest implementation of Creditcoin. The reason is that it uses the chain metadata before creating transactions to be sent and checks for compatibility and remember that gluwa-bot automatically updates the chain metadata whenever required. A side effect of this bot is that updating the Creditcoin version number also changes the metadata. All of this resulted in a CI job which would check the compatibility between the blockchain and our devel tools so that we know they are always usable and in-sync with one another!

As part of the community testing process on Testnet, the development accounts Alice and Bob have been defunded to prevent abuse, for example, stealing funds. By default Alice also has sudo privileges. This defunding broke upgrade and integration testing against a live target. Since then the testing process has started to use different accounts, whose credentials are defined externally and kept out of the CI execution environment due to security concerns. I guess you can't take for granted that certain accounts and pre-conditions will always hold true unless you can control them directly.

As part of the PoW-PoS migration preparation, the team had been exercising using a staging environment. This staging environment initially got stuck after we tried executing the PoW to PoS migration process on it. The reason was that when calling the `switch_to_pos()` extrinsic, it expects a list of accounts which would act as initial validators before the first election cycle is complete. That list expects two entries for each validator – a stash and a controller account – which were then passed down to the BABE pallet (the pallet producing new blocks). The order in which these arguments were specified in the source code was reversed, compared to the order in which BABE expects them. During previous testing, we've always used the same account for both stash and controller, so we didn't see this bug. In terms of "testing," the staging environment did its job to catch the problem.

A side note: "stash" and "controller" is a concept that comes from the Substrate framework where one account, the "controller," acts on behalf of another one, the "stash." During the time of migration, Substrate had already published new versions of the framework migrating from stash + controller accounts to a single account only because using two is confusing. In Creditcoin 3.0 there's only a "stash account! The fact that everyone on the engineering team knew this was part of the reason why no one thought about testing with two different accounts, including yours truly.

Another set of two problems related to migrations was discovered with the staging environment, both of which were almost certain to bring down the entire blockchain. Both are related to a particular block number simply because that number has been used as a hard-coded, large-enough value:

1. An initial problem was found where nodes were running out of memory and crashing. This was happening after a runtime upgrade. That operation was trying to allocate too much memory and was crashing the node. Machines with large enough memory were not crashing, but the upgrade was still taking too much time to be considered viable.

2. The next problem is adjacent – the on_initialize() hook, which executes on every block, was trying to remove too many items from storage. This is the same function which in Creditcoin 2.0 was found to be too eager reading items from on-chain storage into memory; see https://github.com/gluwa/creditcoin/pull/1253 . The current problem was that there were too many items to remove and the

I/O operation took more time than the allowed time in which new blocks must be proposed therefore breaking block production. This is the ::clear_prefix(block_number, u32::MAX, None) code snippet trying to remove an obscenely huge number of items. This fix is in https://github.com/gluwa/creditcoin/pull/1353 – set a limit on how much you can remove per block and spread out the internal cleanup process over multiple blocks.

Few important lessons learned on the testing side:

1. When you see things like u32::MAX, question the hell out of them, and make your CI tools trigger on similar patterns. Nothing good ever comes out of trying to push a software system to its limits.

2. Read/write operations should have limits, and those limits must be verified before they become too large to break the system. In the Substrate framework, in particular it is very easy to read items from on-chain storage and then iterate over them – the code for this is super elegant and easy to use. However, this also means it is very easy to forget an upper limit and try to read too much data into memory.

3. Beware of hard-coded "large-enough" values used in documentation, examples, and test suites because these are the places where your users will look for references if they don't quite know what they are doing and not being careful. If possible try having static tools that trigger on hard-coded numerical values.

The only reason the abovementioned issues were ever close to becoming a big problem on production is that someone was likely told to use an example which was never intended for production purposes. Not knowing and probably not understanding what the example entails, they've copied a value that at the time probably appeared too far away into the future. Kind of like the year 2000 problem programmers had to deal with in the past.

These problems would have never been discovered if the staging environment wasn't forked from production or if it had too few blocks (data in storage). This goes to show how important testing with your production data is! Also goes to show that good developer experience, for example, documentation and quality examples, can benefit both vendor and community developers directly.

Another problem that was discovered was with off-chain worker nonce management. Remember this is the component which talks to the outside world and a nonce is a unique number used during communications. The issue is that when a verification fails the off-chain worker still updates its nonce while the on-chain nonce doesn't change. The off-chain worker can handle the situation when it sends a transaction and that transaction fails immediately, but there's no way to check what's the status of a transaction if it gets removed from the pool at some later time or doesn't fail immediately. So you end up with several failure scenarios on the next round:

- OCW nonce is too small; on-chain nonce is higher – transaction will fail b/c the nonce has already been used.

- Two transactions with the same nonce in the transaction pool – one will be dropped from the pool, but you don't know that it has been dropped. There are also other reasons transactions can be dropped from the transaction pool, and then the two nonce counters get out of sync.

- OCW nonce is too high; on-chain nonce is smaller – transaction looks good, but it stays in the transaction pool "forever." Transaction from the pool will not be included in a block because it is waiting until the on-chain nonce counter catches up to it. The transaction will likely expire before that happens.

This issue has always been present; however, with the switch to proof of stake, the Creditcoin team also added more extrinsics which require off-chain work. The voting process with proof of stake generates lots more on-chain activity, even when there are no loan transactions compared to an idle proof-of-work chain. Both of these facts combined made the problem appear more frequently.

The technical fix for this is to monitor when these counters are about to diverge into a non-recoverable state and reset them.

Testing Challenges During v2.3

I've seen a few challenges during the development phase of v2.3. I believe most of them stem from the rapid development process and the lack of full understanding of all of the involved components. Sounds like any other testing project, right?

Starting with all third-party components and forks – before making any choices and going ahead with implementation we should have taken the time to inspect their upstream code base, state of test suite, CI jobs history, and overall testing practices. As it happened, every single third-party component which we forked was in a rather poor state with regard to testing which opens a whole lot of questions around long-term maintenance. A tricky thing here which had misled the team was that other more popular blockchains are also built on top of the same components.

CHAPTER 6   CREDITCOIN 2.3

After examining the state of the upstream repositories, I do not believe that what's published on GitHub is exactly the same code base used in production. At least not for all of the components involved anyway.

There is no good alternative here though. If the team had decided that these upstream components are not good enough, then we would have needed to invest much more time in developing our own or going through timely discussions with third-party vendors to use their hosted services instead. That's something which works as a long-term strategy and the team will probably do it anyway, but it doesn't work short term when you have a rapid development cycle.

Tip Assert on the state of any critical third-party open source components that you may rely upon! Even when the component doesn't initially appear to be that critical!

The next challenges are related – not understanding the components requirements well enough, due to not being familiar with all of the components themselves, and not communicating detailed enough with stakeholders around their expectations toward the release schedule and perceived level of quality. In practice the "public testnet release" was very close to the actual mainnet release in terms of schedule and quality. For this Testnet release, it wasn't expected that it would be beta quality, rather it was expected that it will be close to production quality with only minor issues and bugs existing. That's different from how other, more traditional software gets developed and published. In other words, the majority of the testing and development pressure gets shifted early in the release lifecycle, and you have sprints which can be roughly classified as periods of high activity and others which are relatively quiet.

In some domains, certainly blockchain and crypto, the appearance of a testing release may very well be more important than the functional quality of said release. This skews the priority of seemingly small issues,

155

which "you may fix later" toward actually becoming a big deal that needs to be addressed quickly and can even block your release. It's all about the optics!

I've mentioned earlier in this book that when relying on third-party components, you need to be aware of who's the vendor producing them and what are their primary business objectives. This is certainly true when directly forking an open source application. For example, the Polkadot Staking Dashboard is used by the Polkadot blockchain, and I've found a number of bugs which they are happy to tolerate. On the other hand, the same bugs are present in the Creditcoin Staking Dashboard fork, and they are viewed as issues that the Creditcoin product owners are less willing to tolerate, therefore necessitating additional investment in development and testing resources in the same area. Simply because a bigger player uses the same underlying software components like you do doesn't mean that the underlying software is 100% top-notch!

Tip Make sure that the entire team understands what's expected quality wise! Make sure engineering and stakeholders are on the same page!

Furthermore, it would be great if we as testers pioneer the adoption of acceptance criteria/release criteria. These are relatively common in large organizations dealing with enterprise-type software but far less so in a fast-moving start-up type of environment.

For example, the Basic Release Criteria for the Fedora Project Linux distribution are documented at https://fedoraproject.org/wiki/Basic_Release_Criteria, and every new feature added inside a particular release has its own additional criteria. I believe this helps align everyone's expectations around what will be delivered and is subject to feedback, planning, and adjustments. It can start small and evolve over time obviously, but I consider the lack of such criteria to be a mistake, especially on my side as a tester.

Migration from PoW to PoS

The actual migration process was scoped out into a document as a checklist and executed several times against different environments: locally, Staging (aka fork of Mainnet) until the team was confident in all the steps and there were no obvious problems before actually migrating Mainnet nodes!

Sadly the `switch_to_pos()` extrinsic, the abovementioned checklist, and all tests related to asserting state before and after the migration from proof of work to proof of stake were no longer needed afterward and have been deleted since. That was really a "one off" type of testing.

Summary

Creditcoin 2.3 obviously survived the switch to proof of stake. At the time of this writing, it has been over 2 million blocks later, so the blockchain has been running as proof of stake longer than it has been running as proof of work. More importantly, I also survived this very hectic period and learned quite a lot more aspects of "testing the blockchain" which I hadn't thought about before.

In the next chapter, I will talk about the next iteration – Creditcoin 3.0 and the novelty it brings onboard. Once again the team makes a switch – this time in a slightly different direction.

CHAPTER 7

Creditcoin 3.0

Creditcoin 3.0 is the next evolution of the Creditcoin blockchain evolving from a specialized blockchain to record loan transactions into a more generic chain targeting real-world asset management. It is a fully EVM-compatible Layer 1 blockchain. In other words, it supports smart-contract development and is compatible with many popular tools used in the Ethereum ecosystem, for example, wallet apps and smart-contract development tools. Creditcoin 3.0 is built with the Substrate framework adding a special EVM compatibility layer on top of it and uses the nominated-proof-of-stake consensus algorithm like its predecessor.

The two main design features are EVM compatibility and the so-called Universal Oracle which unlocks multi-chain information streams and cross-chain transactions to help build and deploy multi-chain contracts. Development work is performed in phases, and at the time of writing this book, only the EVM compatibility layer has been implemented.

Creditcoin 3.0 is proposed as an independent blockchain, rather than an incremental upgrade from the 2.x family which again greatly simplifies development and testing. The original proposal also states that Creditcoin 2 functionality will be implemented as an L2 on Creditcoin 3.0. I am assuming that would be a [set of] smart-contract(s) able to record the loan cycle flow. At the time of writing, these implementation details are non-existent though.

CHAPTER 7   CREDITCOIN 3.0

> **Note**   The public announcement of Creditcoin 3.0 Testnet [1] also mentions renaming of existing blockchains. The previous Creditcoin 2 will be renamed to *"Creditcoin Classic,"* and the new EVM-compatible v3.0 will simply be named *"Creditcoin."* I will keep using explicit version numbers throughout the rest of this book in order to avoid confusion.

Components of Creditcoin 3.0

I am going to outline the most important components of Creditcoin 3.0 here. As it is a Substrate-based chain, some of the items are kind of the same as with Creditcoin 2.

Polkadot-sdk

This is the core Substrate framework used to build the blockchain as described previously. In versions newer than the one used for Creditcoin 2, upstream maintainers have decided to merge several git repositories together and archive the old ones. This is the new name.

Creditcoin 3.0 uses a fork which originally follows the release-polkadot-v1.1.0 branch adding a few patches on top of it.

Source: https://github.com/gluwa/polkadot-sdk

---

[1] https://creditcoin.org/blog/creditcoins-real-world-evm-testnet-is-live/

CHAPTER 7 CREDITCOIN 3.0

Frontier

This is an Ethereum compatibility layer for Substrate providing additional pallets which you may include in a runtime implementation. This component allows each Substrate account to automatically have a so-called "associated EVM address" which can be used for any EVM-related transactions. This is the component which provides EVM Compatibility and allows blockchain users to deploy smart contracts on Creditcoin 3.0. This is how it looks like.

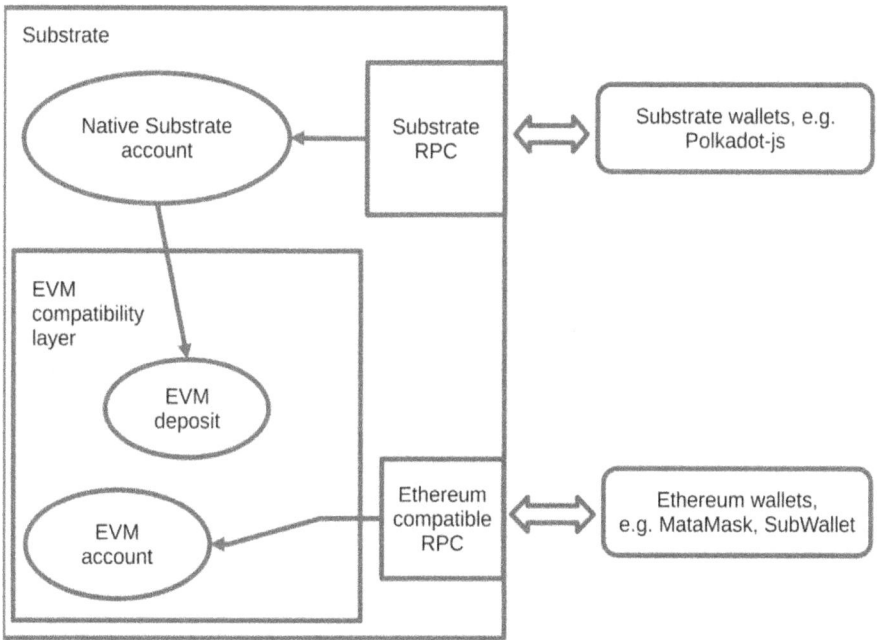

Figure 7-1. EVM compatibility inside a Substrate-based chain

An important note here is that Substrate and Ethereum use different address formats and the addresses are of different lengths too. Ethereum addresses start with the prefix "0x," while Substrate ones don't (and they always start with a 5). Ethereum style addresses are 20 bytes long, while

161

Substrate ones are 32 bytes. This is why in Creditcoin 3.0 each account has two different addresses – the native Substrate address and a virtual EVM address which is called an associated address.

Source: https://github.com/gluwa/frontier

Creditcoin3

This is the main source code repository for the 3.0 version which contains the blockchain runtime implementation, the Docker container specification, and a few other bits. The main difference with Creditcoin 2 is that the majority of this repository is plumbing code – at the time of writing, there are no custom pallets, no custom transactions, and almost no additional RPC calls.

Source: https://github.com/gluwa/creditcoin3

EVM Tracing RPC

This is an internal component, part of the creditcoin3-node client which exports a number of RPC methods capable of tracing through the transactions which have occurred on the EVM layer inside of a Substrate-based chain, for example, transactions inside smart-contracts. The main purpose of this component is to expose the information necessary for block explorers such as Blockscout. Without this, a block explorer application will still be able to see each block and the transactions recorded inside of it; however, it won't be able to traverse inside of the EVM-related transactions and display more granular details about them.

The code for these RPCs comes from the Moonbeam blockchain and has been merged inside of the creditcoin3-node in https://github.com/gluwa/creditcoin3/pull/169. Because this is a very large chunk of third-party code, it has been manually vetted that it performs as expected. Initially the RPC methods exposed by this component were conditionally enabled via a compiler flag and afterward have been included as part of the standard build.

Precompile(s)

This is a component internal to the gluwa/creditcoin3 repository which was added after the official announcement of the Creditcoin 3 Testnet. This component allows you to bridge the gap between the Ethereum side of Creditcoin 3 and the Substrate runtime and interact with the runtime from the EVM side which isn't normally possible.

From an external point of view, this component acts as a smart-contract which is always available at a fixed address, a sort of a predefined collection of smart-contract(s). Implementation wise there is an entry-function which is written in Rust and is part of the Creditcoin runtime. This is very similar to an extrinsics function. Then there is the smart-contract interface definition written in the Solidity language. The important part here is the predefined address at which the contract is going to be deployed.

At the time of writing this book, Creditcoin 3 contains a single precompile called substrate-transfer, whose goal is to make it easier to fund EVM addresses on Creditcoin from existing Substrate wallets in just a single step (otherwise that would take two steps). It is available at address 0x0000000000000000000000000000000000000Fd1 ➤ https://creditcoin-testnet.blockscout.com/address/0x0000000000000000000000000000000000000Fd1

A counter example which contains more precompiled contracts is the Moonbeam network; see https://docs.moonbeam.network/builders/pallets-precompiles/precompiles/ and https://github.com/moonbeam-foundation/moonbeam/tree/master/precompiles for more details.

Creditcoin 3 CLI

Similar to the Creditcoin 2 version, this is a command line program packaged inside the container image and meant to be used by operators of validator nodes. It is part of the gluwa/creditcoin3 git repository. This component started as a copy of the existing command line source code for Creditcoin 2 with two important extras: commands to handle evm transfers + support of proxy functionality.

Proxy Functionality

This is a functional sub-component of both the blockchain and the command line application. I am mentioning it here because it is important and because it affects how we do testing in a major way.

Remember that when talking about Creditcoin 2.3, I've mentioned something called "stash" and "controller" accounts and that it was deprecated. Proxy accounts is the new kid on the block.

As the name suggests in Creditcoin 3.0, users can create another account which holds enough funds to pay transaction fees and to be used for day-to-day operations on behalf of their primary account. Proxies get authorized by the primary account and are then used to sign transactions on behalf of the primary account. Using proxy accounts can significantly reduce the risk of compromising a significant amount of funds in case credentials are accidentally revealed or stolen because the primary account, holding all of the funds, needs to perform a single interaction with the blockchain – authorize the proxy. All other subsequent transactions can be performed using the proxy account secrets, thus minimizing exposure for the primary account.

In a Substrate-based chain, it is possible to implement a proxy filter which exports different proxy types to the user and controls which runtime calls, aka extrinsics, are allowed. This is how you can implement access control for the proxy accounts. Creditcoin 3 comes with three different proxy types: Staking, NonTransfer, and All! This is how filtering is defined for Creditcoin (Listing 7-1).

Listing 7-1. Proxy filter implementation

```
impl InstanceFilter<RuntimeCall> for ProxyFilter {
    fn filter(&self, call: &RuntimeCall) -> bool {
        match self {
            ProxyFilter::All => true,
            ProxyFilter::Staking => matches!(
                call,
                RuntimeCall::Staking(_)
                    | RuntimeCall::Session(_)
                    | RuntimeCall::Utility(_)
                    | RuntimeCall::VoterList(_)
            ),
            ProxyFilter::NonTransfer => matches!(
                call,
                RuntimeCall::Grandpa(_)
                    | RuntimeCall::ImOnline(_)
                    | RuntimeCall::Proxy(_)
                    | RuntimeCall::Session(_)
                    | RuntimeCall::Staking(_)
                    | RuntimeCall::System(_)
                    | RuntimeCall::Timestamp(_)
                    | RuntimeCall::Utility(_)
                    | RuntimeCall::VoterList(_)
            ),
        }
    }
}
```

```
fn is_superset(&self, o: &Self) -> bool {
    match (self, o) {
        (ProxyFilter::All, _) => true,
        (ProxyFilter::NonTransfer, ProxyFilter::Staking)
            => true,
        (a, b) if a == b => true,
        _ => false,
    }
}
```

Staking Dashboard

This is a web application which allows nominators to stake their funds and vote for validators. It is a standard React.js application which connects wallet browser extensions, for example, SubWallet to the Creditcoin 3 blockchain. The main functionality of Creditcoin Staking Dashboard is staking funds, filtering and voting for validators, creating and participating in nomination pools, and monitoring past performance and rewards.

The origin of Staking Dashboard for Creditcoin 3 begins with the existing Creditcoin Staking Dashboard for v2 of the chain. Originally, we were thinking that a rebase to the latest available from the upstream fork will be enough to support both versions of the blockchain. The raw commits are in https://github.com/gluwa/creditcoin-staking-dashboard/pull/108.

While working on this rebase, the team actually established that the upstream codebase has evolved to the point that it actually required an updated version of the Substrate framework used to build the blockchain. Luckily the amount of incompatibilities wasn't very high, and it was technically possible to support both versions of Creditcoin using a single instance of Staking Dashboard; see the last commit on PR #108.

Whether or not the arrangement of supporting multiple chains which have different versions within a single code base of Staking Dashboard would have worked is anybody's guess. It very likely would have led to some sort of compatibility issue down the line. We will never know because a decision was made to spin off the existing code into a new repository, called gluwa/creditcoin3-staking-dashboard, and continue development separately. In production the two instances of Staking Dashboard are separate, and they are hosted under different URLs.

Public URL: https://cc3-staking.creditcoin.org

Source: https://github.com/gluwa/creditcoin3-staking-dashboard/

Subscan API

Subscan is an API service which monitors dozens of Substrate-based blockchain networks and aggregates information into a SQL database. This component is used by the Staking Dashboard for the purposes of rendering performance charts, for example, past rewards. It also provides a certain level of block-explorer functionality.

This is the same component as in Creditcoin 2.3; however, instead of using it as an open source fork, Creditcoin 3 uses a SaaS version of this API publicly accessible at https://creditcoin3-testnet.subscan.io/.

Blockscout

Blockscout is a tool for inspecting and analyzing EVM-based blockchains aka a blockchain explorer. The main difference between Blockscout and other explorers, such as Subscan, is that it understands smart-contract calls or so-called internal transactions. In other words, transactions which aren't represented by the existing Substrate extrinsics.

This component is consumed as a service, and Creditcoin 3.0's Testnet explorer can be found at https://creditcoin-testnet.blockscout.com/.

Crunch

In a NPoS blockchain based on the Substrate framework, validators and nominators earn rewards in the form of crypto tokens. This happens in every era, and there is a maximum window in which such rewards may be paid out – 84 eras. Anyone can trigger a payout but that doesn't happen automatically.

Crunch is a command-line interface and a Matrix bot to claim staking rewards every era for Substrate-based chains, thus reducing the need for manual interactions with the blockchain.

This component is a fork of `turboflakes/crunch` with changes specific to Creditcoin 3.0 and in particular with the intention to be used for automatically requesting payouts earned by Gluwa's own validator nodes. It is written in the Rust programming language.

Source: `https://github.com/gluwa/crunch`

Timeline of Creditcoin 3.0

This book outlines testing activities from the initial creation of 3.0 repositories until shortly after the public announcement of Creditcoin 3.0 Testnet – roughly between December 2023 and May 2024.

Creditcoin 3 Testnet was officially announced on March 21, 2024![2]

Testing of Creditcoin 3.0

Testing for the 3.0 version largely builds upon the experience gained during testing the 2.x family of Creditcoin. This means things like static analysis tools, external and internal linters, and automatic updates, for example, Dependabot, are basically the same as in previous version.

---

[2] https://creditcoin.org/blog/creditcoins-real-world-evm-testnet-is-live/

CHAPTER 7   CREDITCOIN 3.0

Because development of Creditcoin 3 began after 99% of the testing practices and infrastructure of Creditcoin 2 was already in place, it was fairly common in the early days to copy all of the CI configuration verbatim from the Creditcoin 2 repository and then adjust bits and pieces where needed. This section will try focusing on what's different in terms of testing for Creditcoin 3.0 instead of repeating all of the items I've mentioned for Creditcoin 2.0 and 2.3 previously.

Keep in mind that one of the main testing objectives for the 3.0 version is EVM compatibility.

Here's how a typical CI pipeline exercised on pull requests looks like (Figure 7-2).

Figure 7-2. *CI jobs overview*

Unit Tests

The Rust code base of Creditcoin 3.0 has a very small number of unit tests predominantly coming from the evm-tracing package. The rest are checks around Ethereum account ID derivation and checking that base extrinsic weight is EVM compatible. Precompiles are similar to extrinsic functions, and they have their own unit tests as well.

CHAPTER 7   CREDITCOIN 3.0

The actual source code inside the `gluwa/creditcoin3` repository, except the evm-tracing package and precompiles/ directory, is mostly the runtime plumbing. There isn't much that can be exercised on the unit test level – there are no custom RPCs or custom metrics, there are no pallets, nor there are custom extrinsics like in Creditcoin 2.

EVM and Smart-Contract Testing

We're using a smart-contract test suite, written by a different team. This test suite is packaged as the `@gluwa/evm-network-test` NPM package and provides a few executable commands as its entry points. At the time of writing this book, there are `basicTest` and `gasTest` commands both of which require a Creditcoin RPC URL and a private key as their arguments.

These commands can be executed as such:

```
./node_modules/.bin/basicTest --rpc <creditcoin-rpc-url>
--private_key <private-key-for-a-funded-account>
```

Note that addresses and private keys here are in the EVM format, starting with 0x, not the Substrate format. For executing against a standalone blockchain running in developer-mode, one can use the pre-funded development accounts and their addresses and private keys which are described in more details on `https://docs.moonbeam.network/builders/get-started/networks/moonbeam-dev/#pre-funded-development-accounts`.

This EVM test suite is executed via Hardhat Runner – a popular task runner, part of a very popular development environment for Ethereum-based smart-contracts called Hardhat. The actual files containing test scenarios are written in JavaScript with the popular `chai` assertion library which is the default in the Hardhat ecosystem.

`baseTest` compiles and deploys a smart contract which represents a crypto token, then exercises various transactions on it, and asserts on the expected state. The focus here is to make sure that a contract representing an ERC20 crypto token can be deployed onto Creditcoin, tokens can be transferred between different wallets, and in general that users can interact with the deployed contract. The `gasTest` tool collects gas results into a CSV file. Despite its name, there are no assertions in this file.

The source code repository for this test suite isn't available via GitHub, but the NPM package, published under the open source MIT license, is available from `https://www.npmjs.com/package/@gluwa/evm-network-test`, and you can examine the actual code after installing it. Just `cd into the node_modules/@gluwa/evm-network-test/ directory and take a look`.

From the blockchain point of view, the tools which are part of this test suite are executed against every environment we run blockchain-related integration tests on, for example, local, Devnet, Testnet, etc. You can think of it as another branch of the integration test suite which is available in the main repository.

Testing EVM Tracing Functionality

The RPC methods `debug_traceTransaction` and `debug_traceBlockByHash` are the entry points to EVM tracing, and they are exercised via an integration test which deploys a smart contract, makes a couple of transactions, and then calls these RPC methods with the respective transactions hashes and asserts on the responses. These two RPC methods are meant to be consumed by third-party providers, so they are considered to be important, and if this test breaks, that will be a major blocker. This isn't a stand-alone test suite but rather just some of the existing scenarios.

CHAPTER 7 CREDITCOIN 3.0

Integration Tests for the Blockchain

This is the parent of any sort of so-called integration testing related to the blockchain itself. It is written in TypeScript and uses the Jest testing framework. Source code location under the gluwa/creditcoin3 repository is `cli/src/test/blockchain-tests`.

> **Note** To make it easier/simpler to reuse shared code and helper functions, the blockchain integration test suite is bundled together with the unit/integration test suite for the Creditcoin 3 CLI component. This saves a bit of effort trying to figure out where everything is and makes the code base simpler. An alternative is moving it into a separate directory and managing dependencies separately which was perceived as extra work without extra benefit.

Similar to Creditcoin 2, this test suite is controlled via Jest config files and can be executed against different environments, including against a production environment. At the time of writing, it includes the aforementioned evm-tracing tests, queries, and asserts on some runtime values from the running chain it is being executed against and exercises the available precompile, substrate_transfer, from the outside.

Another important mention here is that Creditcoin 3 is more diverse when it comes to configuration for different environments. The major difference is in block time and staking epoch duration which are different for local, Devnet, and Testnet.

Precompile Testing

This was already mentioned, but it deserves a separate section because there's more in this area. Obviously there are unit and integration tests which cover positive and negative path scenarios. There is also something else, called contract metadata.

This metadata is stored in JSON files, and the Blockscout explorer application reads these JSON files via their URL. That's necessary so that Blockscout knows what additional information to display for this contract when analyzing internal transactions related to it.

This metadata contains the precompile name, address, its bytecode, as well as 1-line version of the Solidity source code. It is treated as an external API interface from the Blockscout application.

On the testing side, I mostly use custom static analysis scripts to assert on things like

- File names don't change b/c that will result in 404 errors and break the consumer application.

- Bytecode and source code included in metadata actually match the Solidity interface definition.

- Addresses are defined in separate JSON fields so they need to match.

- We already know how to automatically update source code in the repository so regenerate metadata in the event the underlying source code changes and commit to git using gluwa-bot.

- The naming convention here is per branch aka per environment (e.g., Devnet, Testnet, Mainnet) so make sure that expected files are available based on which branch we are releasing into and roll forward the aforementioned automatic source updates according to the existing release procedures.

- The existing integration tests use the ethers.js library which needs the contract hex address and the contract ABI, Application Binary Interface, in the form of another JSON file before it can instantiate an object that interacts with the blockchain. Obviously these two pieces of information are hard-coded, but we need to make sure that they always match the origin source code and don't diverge over time, that is, not testing exactly the same piece of code that you are building!

The question which is still unclear to me at the time of this writing is what do we have to do in case there are more precompiled contracts added to the blockchain. Do we squash all of their metadata into the same JSON file, or do we start having individual files per contract? The answer to this question will have an impact on how checks are performed.

Testing Creditcoin 3 CLI and Proxy Functionality

For Creditcoin 3 CLI, there is the expected combination of unit tests asserting against various helper functions which don't require a running chain and integration tests which exercise individual commands and the validator flow and assert on their successful execution, expected error handling, and on-chain state. The existing test suite here is more detailed compared to the Creditcoin 2 cli test suite. I've intentionally added tests for every single command supported by the command line application, exercising both positive and negative scenarios as well as a couple of end-to-end test scenarios.

Because each testing scenario is executed independently, I've given up on trying to collect and combine code coverage metrics. Instead I've analyzed test coverage for each command and added the missing ones. This isn't as terrible as it sounds because the set of available commands almost doesn't change past their initial introduction – doing the test coverage analysis by hand is acceptable in such a situation in my opinion. This time I've gone for a low-tech solution instead looking to automate.

A notable difference for Creditcoin 3 CLI test suite is exercising proxy functionality as part of the test suite. We have to consider the following attributes:

- Are we using proxy account? Yes or No.

- Is the supplied proxy account secret valid? Yes; No; Yes, but the account has no funds; Yes, but the proxy has been configured for a different account

- What is the proxy type? Three possible values

Implementation wise, using proxy accounts results in a few important differences:

1. Any secrets handling code must ask for the proxy account secrets, not for the stash account ones.

2. Signing and submitting transactions to the blockchain must be done via the proxy account.

3. Checking available balance is twofold:

    1. Proxy account must have enough funds to pay fees.

    2. Any additional amount must be checked against the stash account balance – for example, when you want to stake more funds, then your primary account, not the proxy account, must have the specified free balance.

4. Displaying balance and status, query operations, must always use the primary account address even when querying the chain via the proxy account.

We're not interested in the case where a supplied secret isn't valid because that will prevent any keyrings from initializing, regardless of whether a proxy account is used or not. This will fail early on before reaching the chain and isn't tested explicitly. Some of the other combinations aren't valid either, so we're left with the following testing combinations which are expressed as environment variables inside of the CI configuration:

1. proxy=no
2. proxy=yes / no-funds /
3. proxy=yes / not-a-proxy /
4. proxy=yes / valid-proxy / type=Staking
5. proxy=yes / valid-proxy / type=NonTransfer
6. proxy=yes / valid-proxy / type=All

For scenarios 2 and 3, the focus is on asserting on the expected error handling. The command line application should not crash, and it should not allow transactions to go through. Instead it should print a human-friendly error message explaining what went wrong. This is something I worked on even after the Testnet announcement because we didn't get it fully correct on the first try.

The test suite uses common setup/teardown functions which manipulate testing accounts, their funds, and/or their secrets accordingly. The majority of the test scenarios inside this test suite make use of conditional execution, utilizing custom functions called `testIf` and `describeIf`, see Listing 7-2. These functions are built upon the existing `test()` and `describe()` functions from the Jest testing framework and execute the actual test scenarios only when the given expression evaluates to true because not every test scenario is applicable to every possible environment combination, for example:

Listing 7-2. Example usage of the `testIf()` function

```
testIf(
    process.env.PROXY_ENABLED === 'yes' && process.env.PROXY_
    SECRET_VARIANT === 'no-funds',
    'should error with account balance too low message',
    () => {
        try {
            CLI('bond --amount 111');
        } catch (error: any) {
            expect(error.exitCode).toEqual(1);
            expect(error.stderr).toContain(
                'Invalid Transaction: Inability to pay some
                fees , e.g. account balance too low',
            );
        }
    },
);
```

Some CLI commands do not support proxy functionality, either by explicit choice or because they don't require the user to be authenticated at all. For such commands, the conditional test execution will evaluate the environment and skip testing when needed instead of duplicating extra executions which will not bring any new information. These commands are primarily tested when proxy=no.

Note that all of these six variants execute in parallel, and because they selectively skip some test scenarios, there isn't much overhead in the overall feedback time when opening a pull request. The longest variant is proxy=no closely followed by all combinations with a valid proxy configuration. The longest test scenario of all is actually `validatorCycle.test.ts` which exercises each individual command in sequence, waits and asserts on the results, distributes rewards, and then stops being a validator, unbonds all funds, waits for them to become available, and then withdraws the funds.

Another dimension of variability added to the entire test suite en-masse was parametrizing the target URL for all cli commands. There are two nodes called Alice and Bob, and which one we talk to is specified as `--url ws://127.0.0.1:<port>`. For the majority of testing scenarios, we piggy-back on the proxy handling code which conveniently inserts the `--url` argument in the resulting command line.

All existing cli commands are covered with tests, and the addition of more test scenarios for each of these commands made the test suite grow to a point at which it actually started to fail because the test automation code had a problem. The short version is that scenarios which were supposed to be independent actually had a shared state, and that was causing side effects to manifest between other test scenarios. In particular, the actual integration testing looked like in Figure 7-3.

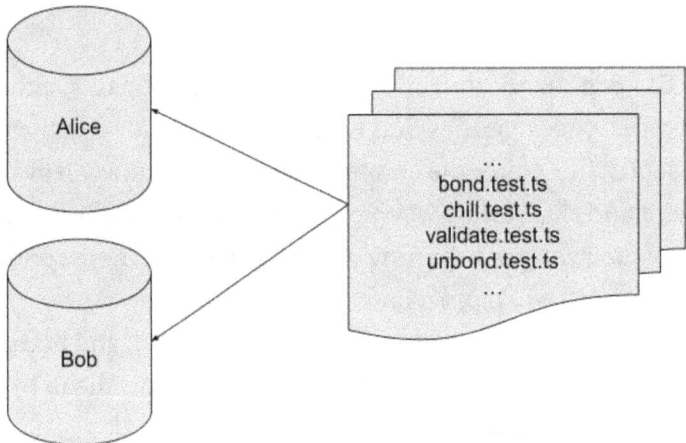

Figure 7-3. *All tests using a shared blockchain*

While the individual `*.test.ts` files are still executed independently of one another, in sequence, the practical implementation was that each test scenario will create a random account on the blockchain and then use it to assume the roles of an active validator and exercise different commands under test with that role. The shared state, for example, who is the active validator and which account controls the nodes Alice and Bob, was recorded on-chain, and it happened that in some situations the blockchain's active validator set was configured with certain accounts, while in reality the next command was executing with a different account.

For example, `validate.test.ts` uses an account XXXXXX to become a validator with Bob's node and then doesn't clean up properly after itself. On the next step, another test scenario generates an account YYYYYY and also tries to become a validator controlling Bob's node! In a sense hijacking the running Creditcoin node without cleaning up properly. That's possible because configuring session keys for the node (e.g., rotate keys) is a permissionless operation, and as long as you have access to the running process (e.g., the RPC port), you can do this.

This results in a state where the on-chain algorithms are expecting certain signatures before they can finalize a block, but those signatures never arrive because the validator accounts are no more. This breaks finalization which in turn breaks all client transactions. More precisely, transactions still make it into new blocks, but our tools, including the test automation suite, are designed to wait until a block is finalized before reporting an error. Because finalization never happens, everything becomes super slow until commands and test jobs eventually time out.

The solution to this problem is actually very simple – make sure test scenarios don't have a shared state – that is, start a new independent chain before every group of test scenarios is executed as shown in Figure 7-4!

CHAPTER 7 CREDITCOIN 3.0

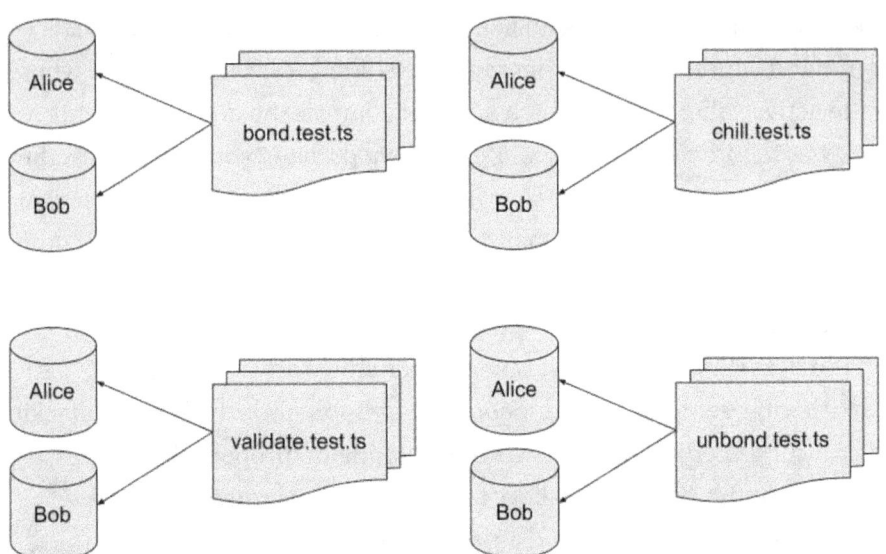

Figure 7-4. *Each test using a dedicated blockchain instance*

The practical side of implementing this separation between individual tests was handled by supplying a custom value for the setupFilesAfterEnv key in Jest's test runner config plus a global beforeAll / afterAll pair to perform the setup and teardown of the individual chains. Worked like a charm and added negligible overhead to total execution time of this test suite.

```
$ cat integration-tests.config.ts
import type { Config } from '@jest/types';

const config: Config.InitialOptions = {
preset: 'ts-jest',
testEnvironment: 'node',
setupFilesAfterEnv: ['./integrationTestSetupAfterEnv.ts'],
};

export default config;

$ cat integrationTestSetupAfterEnv.ts
```

```
global.beforeAll(async () => {
await startAliceAndBob();
}, 10_000);

global.afterAll(() => {
killCreditcoinNodes();
});
```

To make sure that the target under test looks sane before executing any commands and asserting on their side effects, the same approach was used. Listing 7-3 shows the global beforeEach() function. This also has the extra benefit of failing early.

Listing 7-3. Implementation of global.beforeEach() setup function

```
global.beforeEach(async () => {
const [last, finalized] = await Promise.all([
     api.rpc.chain.getBlock(),
     api.rpc.chain.getBlock(await api.rpc.chain.
     getFinalizedHead()),
]);

const lastBlockNumber = last.block.header.number.toNumber();
const lastFinalizedNumber = finalized.block.header.number.
toNumber();

expect(lastBlockNumber - lastFinalizedNumber).
toBeLessThanOrEqual(5);
});
```

The function startAliceAndBob spawns two background processes and also captures stdout and stderr into text files which are later uploaded as CI artifacts in case you need to debug failures. That functionality became handy during implementation of the global.beforeEach hook. The api variable, not shown in the listing for brevity, is created within the same function and always connects to Alice. The reason is that this code snippet executes before any real test scenarios take place, and we cannot access context variables in said test scenarios. After around eight test files were executed, everything started failing randomly in CI but not locally. The reason turned out to be a networking issue, and no new connections were going through. This is how it looked like (Listing 7-4).

Listing 7-4. Failure output from the integration test suite

```
PASS src/test/integration-tests/validate.test.ts (285.371 s)
validate
    ✓ should error when current bond < MinValidatorBond
      (105372 ms)
  when NOT bonded
    ✓ should error with staking.NotController message
      (62097 ms)
  when ALREADY bonded
    ✓ should become a waiting validator (94698 ms)
  ○ skipped should error with account balance too low message
    ○ skipped should error with proxy.NotProxy message

PASS src/test/integration-tests/unbond.test.ts (155.562 s)
unbond
  when NOT bonded
    ✓ should error with validator not bonded message
      (46586 ms)
  when ALREADY bonded
    ✓ should be able to unbond (100319 ms)
    ○ skipped should error with account balance too low message
    ○ skipped should error with proxy.NotProxy message

FAIL src/test/integration-tests/evm.test.ts (254.119 s)
EVM Commands
  EVM Fund
```

✓ should be able to fund an EVM account (31576 ms)
✓ should not be able to fund more than existing funds
  (15386 ms)

EVM Withdraw
  ✓ should be able to withdraw CTC to a Substrate account
    via --url ws://127.0.0.1:9944 (44660 ms)
  ✓ should be able to withdraw CTC to a Substrate account
    via --url ws://127.0.0.1:9955 (44010 ms)

EVM Balance
  ✗ should be able to show evm balance correctly when balance
    is zero (100112 ms)
  ✗ should be able to show balance correctly after funding
    (10001 ms)

● EVM Commands › EVM Balance › should be able to show evm
balance correctly when balance is zero
thrown: "Exceeded timeout of 100000 ms for a hook.
Add a timeout value to this test to increase the timeout,
if this is a long-running test. See https://jestjs.io/docs/
api#testname-fn-timeout".

The actual bug was that my helper function did not call `api.disconnect()`. How did I debug this?

1. All test files are executed sequentially, so I counted which one was the first to fail. I was interested in the number, not the actual test file, and this number stayed very consistent between different CI executions.

2. Then downloaded all log files from CI artifacts – their names include the Alice or Bob pattern and a timestamp, see Listing 7-5.

Listing 7-5. Names of log files from multiple parallel test jobs

```
creditcoin3-node-Alice-2024-04-03T10-01-55.594Z-log.stderr
creditcoin3-node-Alice-2024-04-03T10-07-22.470Z-log.stderr
creditcoin3-node-Alice-2024-04-03T10-12-03.658Z-log.stderr
creditcoin3-node-Alice-2024-04-03T10-16-49.086Z-log.stderr
```

3. Found the files for both Alice and Bob corresponding to the execution number in which I was seeing failures, I think it was 8, and started looking into them. Because each test now uses a stand-alone blockchain, these files aren't very big.

4. I started reading the log files, top to bottom. Everything looked good in terms of block production when suddenly I saw the error message shown in Listing 7-6:

Listing 7-6. Error message shown in creditcoin3-node logs

```
2024-04-03 10:22:06 Too many connections. Please try again later.
```

I suspect that locally my OS was able to recycle TCP connections much faster compared to the containerized runners used by GitHub Actions, and/or their environment was much more limited in terms of how many TCP ports are available. Once I added the call to .disconnect(), everything was fine!

Runtime Upgrade Testing

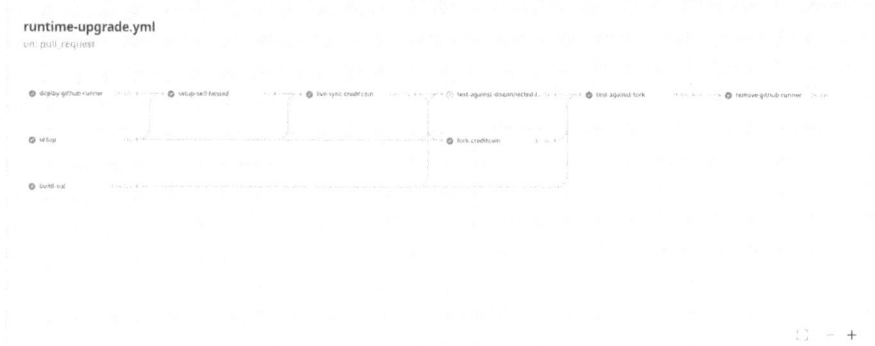

Figure 7-5. *Runtime upgrade CI pipeline*

Contrary to Creditcoin 2, there are no custom storage migrations because there are no custom pallets in Creditcoin 3. This removes the need for all of the plumbing around testing and asserting on migrations described previously. So no try-runtime, no assertions against items in storage before and after migrations, and no special macros to crash the node in case a migration goes south!

There is still the need to perform a runtime upgrade and check whether the chain continues to function as before. This also somewhat covers any possible system migrations that may exist. The process for this is very similar to Creditcoin 2 as shown in Figure 7-5 – synchronize with a live chain, fork, and upgrade and test (blockchain + smart contract tests).

Testing Creditcoin Staking Dashboard

Everything that was said previously for Staking Dashboard and the lack of a comprehensive test suite from the upstream repository still holds true. As a result this component relies heavily on being manually tested which requires a connection to a running chain.

Quite often I'd run a local Creditcoin node using our `fast-runtime` compiler flag, to make staking periods shorter, and then checkout a pull request and execute `yarn dev` in order to review and test the new changes proposed for Staking Dashboard. Under the hood this component is a static JavaScript single-page application. To make it easier for myself and others to be able to review pull requests, I instrumented the build process to copy the static files into cloud storage and then post a comment on the pull request (Figure 7-6).

Figure 7-6. *Ephemeral preview as GitHub comment*

Clicking on the *"Staking Dashboard Preview"* link will open a URL, which is unique for every pull request and hosts the application as built from the latest commit in that pull request. I call it an *ephemeral deployment* or a *preview build*, but there isn't much of an actual deployment here – it's just HTML and JavaScript.

This also builds the application under test in development mode so that the connection *"CreditcoinLocal"* is displayed in the menu. This allows the tester to easily use Creditcoin Staking Dashboard while running a local blockchain accessible at ws://127.0.0.1:9944. Alternatively you can also connect to other environments like Devnet and Testnet if the bug was only reproducible in one of them.

Super small technical contribution, see `https://github.com/gluwa/creditcoin3-staking-dashboard/pull/34`, which actually provides a great productivity boost so I will definitely continue doing this in the future.

As can be expected, the upstream polkadot-staking-dashboard code base also contains issues and bugs that negatively affect downstream forks, for example, https://github.com/paritytech/polkadot-staking-dashboard/issues/2031. Another one I found myself personally is the inability to display current configuration for nomination pool commission once set. Opening the corresponding modal widget the next time around shows a blank screen as if nothing had been configured. After digging through the relevant sections of Substrate's source code, it looks to me like this functional area isn't feature complete, and there were some commits which to me indicate that an access control model around who can configure nomination pools commission will be implemented in future versions. If that's the case, it would explain why this widget in Staking Dashboard looks rough around the edges.

While we can report such issues upstream, patch them downstream, and even contribute said patches upstream, we should recognize the fact that there is zero guarantee any of this will be accepted by the maintainers. While graciously providing their code base as open source, it is important to recognize that Polkadot is in the business of building a Web3 platform and are in fact a direct competitor. They are not necessarily a software vendor or a traditional open source project, and changes to their code base are most likely accepted if they align with their own long-term vision and goals. As demonstrated several times in other parts of this book, this has an impact on downstream consumers such as Creditcoin.

Indeed during the writing of this book, there were some breaking changes upstream, and an important piece from the Polkadot ecosystem, a UI application similar to Staking Dashboard, had one of their pages updated so that it only works with newer compatible chains. That was the Staking page. As it turns out, the issue was reported immediately by Polkadex which, from the attached screenshots, appear to be using the Polkadot JS Apps as part of their user interface; see https://github.com/polkadot-js/apps/issues/10505. As of this writing, this upstream issue was seeking guidance on what the expected path forward would be and whether there will be some sort of backward compatibility provided. As it stands, during the time writing this section, this upstream change has the potential to affect several of Creditcoin's downstream components. The same goes on for other blockchains relying on the same upstream code base!

Not only does this change have an impact on production deployments, but it also has an impact on testing – the Polkadot JS Apps UI is a convenient way of exploring and monitoring blockchains, especially local ones while performing testing activities. The effective disappearance of an entire page in this application, especially the one related to all staking activities, makes it impossible to observe anything related to this area making downstream testing that much harder. Luckily the non-development instance, actually an older version, of this app still shows the Staking page when connected to a non-compatible chain (aka an older chain) and is a viable workaround for testing purposes, until this older version gets removed from the Internet that is. Hosted at `https://ipfs.io/ipfs/Qmd5YFzh6CqnJJJyQ9FWYff9SDSP2mmj8oTqgBaQz8uWwV/#/staking`.

Note that this URL represents an older production version and may have expired since then.

Do you remember the Subscan API service? While migrating to a SaaS service transfers any concerns around quality and testing for this component toward its vendor, it introduces a slightly undesirable side effect – you cannot test certain functionalities of the Staking Dashboard application because they rely on consuming SaaS APIs which are not available for all environments. Certainly not available when running a development blockchain on localhost. For example, data about nomination pool members comes from the Subscan API service. As a result of this service not being available for 127.0.0.1 Creditcoin Staking Dashboard displays zero members and an empty list in the corresponding UI widget!

While you can test using an arbitrary Staking Dashboard deployment connected to other blockchain environments, for example, Devnet, Testnet, and even Mainnet (all of them have their corresponding Subscan API SaaS endpoints), you simply cannot test against CreditcoinLocal even when connected to it! Depending on the technical details of certain features, this may prove to be either just a nuisance or escalate to a larger test blocker. Something to keep in mind when using third-party services!

Testing Gluwa's Polkadot-sdk Fork

Like any other upstream fork, I follow the mantra *"enable all CI jobs and tests that already exist and then some more."* Which in the case with polkadot-sdk isn't much – couple documentation checks and linters and rustfmt. Similar to the older upstream repository for Substrate, this one has most of its upstream test jobs inside of a private GitLab CI instance which is not exactly easy to replicate downstream. The definition file is still inside of the git repository, but it heavily depends on private docker images and resources.

Again the minimum of enabling branch protection rules, lint, build, and execute the existing unit tests was in order. The CI config uses self-hosted GitHub runners deployed on the fly, and execution time takes between 5 and 6 hours. It is a big test suite! In fact this repository is so big that even trying to compile the source code is impossible on my laptop. It takes around couple of hours before it actually crashes because I don't have enough memory available! 32 gigs ought to be enough for everyone ?!?

Testing Gluwa's Frontier Fork

This fork is much better in terms of existing upstream tests and CI configuration inside a downstream repository. It was just a matter of enabling GitHub Actions on the fork and configuring branch protection rules. It is small enough that it doesn't need a self-hosted GitHub runner.

CHAPTER 7   CREDITCOIN 3.0

Testing Gluwa's Crunch Fork

This is probably the worst example of lack of testing both upstream and downstream which I've seen in a while. Or maybe I am just biased because I want everything to have tests.

Upstream includes pipeline configuration only for releases and that's triggered only on git tags. They will execute the available unit test suite via `cargo test` and proceed to build and upload the binary artifacts. At the time of writing, the upstream repository `turboflakes/crunch` has less than 10 unit tests, no linting configuration whatsoever, and doesn't build with older versions of `rustc`.

Downstream the situation isn't much better, and existing test scenarios related to configuration are actually failing as of commit f29129d12f9ba6c03d67b450b39f1eba3782bc6d.

Note that at the time of writing I had not been involved with the crunch component, and configuring its CI jobs, tooling, and branch protection rules is something yet to be done in the future. Sometimes it does feel like I'm spending more time dealing with sub-optimal testing and code quality coming from upstream instead of focusing on actually testing behavior for the products we build.

Documentation Review and Third-Party Tools Testing

As you can imagine, the documentation for Creditcoin v3 started as a fork of the existing documentation for Creditcoin 2.3 and was then amended with information about the EVM compatibility layer and guides for deploying smart contracts. The initial content creation was done by the devel team and proofread by QA. Some pages of the documentation contain command line or source code examples, in particular the **Smart-Contract Guides** section. This naturally begs the question: how do we make sure that these examples are always up to date? I will even go a stretch further and ask: *how do we test third-party visual tools*, for example, deploying smart contracts via Remix – a popular IDE for Ethereum or via the command line tool Hardhat?

Remember that a similar use case with original programming examples on Creditcoin 2.0 was how the creditcoin-js library was born. Subsequently this library took a life of its own.

Checking code examples, documentation, and instructions for third-party tools may not seem important from a functional point of view – after all this isn't your source code. However, when your core functionality becomes the ability to support smart contracts, then your main customer becomes the blockchain developer or wanna-be developer, and it is critical to at least make sure that the tools you advertise work acceptably. We can think about it along the lines of interoperability testing and being aware of potential known issues, which, while not your fault, may negatively impact user experience.

While writing this book, I had started exercising these third-party tools and found out that in the case of Hardhat the tool has evolved fast enough that some of the commands and the examples provided in the Creditcoin documentation were already considered deprecated. Installing the latest version of Hardhat and following the documentation verbatim simply did not work. That's why all of these examples were moved under git and the commands exercised via CI job. Documentation was updated to point to the example content via its URL so that readers can copy the most up-to-date version.

Documentation URL: `https://docs.creditcoin.org/` (different from the Creditcoin 2.0+ docs)

CHAPTER 7   CREDITCOIN 3.0

Other Interesting Testing

> **Tip** Any third-party tools and dependencies that you use, even if only as part of your development, testing, and/or release pipelines can fail if you pursue an aggressive upgrade strategy.

In the case of Creditcoin and the Rust programming language, some tools and packages require a newer compiler version, for example, https://github.com/gluwa/creditcoin3/pull/159. It's fine when you know that and can wait for all of the relevant bits to be upgraded. This becomes an issue when you have extra dependencies, not directly specified in Cargo.toml, the Rust package manager files, but rather installed directly into CI jobs using fixed versions. To make the matter worse, the CI job which failed is executed conditionally and of course not as part of the pull request updating the compiler version! To make the matter even worse, the subwasm package, the culprit that failed, on crates.io, the Rust package repository, is 3 years old; new versions have made it only as git tags and cannot benefit from the automated Dependabot upgrades.

All in all, it's a lesson in testing – everything that you use needs to be tested. If it isn't included as part of existing CI jobs/test suites, then you need to make sure it is exercised explicitly! Otherwise it is just going to fail when you least expect; see https://github.com/gluwa/creditcoin3/pull/332. At the time of this writing, I had to upgrade from v0.17.1 to v0.19.0 to avoid compiler errors. Even this version isn't 100% happy. It produces a compiler warning:

```
warning: ambiguous glob re-exports
  --> lib/src/lib.rs:19:9
   |
19 | pub use chain_info::*;
```

```
   |         ^^^^^^^^^^^^ the name `Error` in the type namespace
   |         is first re-exported here
...
24 | pub use types::*;
   |         -------- but the name `Error` in the type namespace is
   |         also re-exported here
   |
   = note: `#[warn(ambiguous_glob_reexports)]` on by default
warning: `subwasmlib` (lib) generated 1 warning
   Compiling subwasm v0.19.0
```

Challenge: How to Analyze and Keep Track of Changes to On-Chain Settings

There is an interesting challenge related to modifying various on-chain, and possibly runtime, configuration settings. If you recall, many of the blockchain parameters are hard-coded in source code under runtime/, and there are many more which can also be changed afterward. For example, using the Polkadot JS Apps web interface, it is very easy to send a nominationPools.setConfig transaction and modify existing configuration – for example, change minimum bond amount required to create a nomination pool. This poses two main challenges:

1. How to keep track of such changes; in other words if I am to wipe out an existing environment and redeploy it with the latest Creditcoin version, how do I make sure that its operational parameters will be the same as before?

2. How do I analyze such changes in order to figure out what are the possible risks of modifying a value on-chain? In https://github.com/paritytech/polkadot-sdk/issues/3739, the upstream

maintainers of polkadot-sdk recommend that blockchain developers be careful when changing values on existing chains to avoid shooting themselves in the foot. Reason being is that existing tests and checks upstream are also not perfect and they could have missed a scenario which would have a negative impact.

The first challenge is relatively easy to solve. Substrate already contains the storage migration sub-component, and I've outlined several testing activities related to migrations. While enabling the whole migrations machinery and testing infrastructure around it just so you can change a single value is an overkill; see, for example, `https://github.com/gluwa/creditcoin3/pull/120`. I believe that this is an important first step in solving both challenges.

Having all on-chain storage changes as part of a migration yields several benefits:

- Everything is in git so history and traceability is preserved.

- Any new environment launched from future code versions will take care to configure itself as needed.

- You can test against mock and production data in order to find edge cases.

- Assuming you know how to solve challenge #2, then you can use the migrations machinery and implement pre-conditions into the source code which will alert you when a migration is about to break, for example, when testing against a production environment before a release.

CHAPTER 7   CREDITCOIN 3.0

On to the bigger challenge – how can you analyze a proposed change in order to gain confidence that nothing would break or that it would not cause unforeseen side effects? For example, we already know that changing block time is a no-go, and there are assertions in place in order to catch such a situation before it makes it through the entire release pipeline. What about other settings, which appear to be benign?

At the time of writing this book, I've been thinking about how to solve this challenge but still don't have the full answer. Because the entirety of Creditcoin comprises several layers and applications I believe whatever analysis you do must encompass all of them. I am also a firm believer that in the face of unknown technology, we should first strive to understand how it works in its core before trying to search edge cases and possible risks. Without in-depth understanding, we're just guessing and that is not good enough in my opinion. The overall process will probably be something like this:

- Find all places, in all applications, or libraries, where a particular storage item/setting value is used.

- Create a list of the different functional areas where it is used, for example, `https://github.com/gluwa/creditcoin3/pull/283#issuecomment-2015201729`, because it may not be immediately obvious or because other developers may have decided to add additional checks in unexpected places.

- Try to understand what all of the areas on your list are doing and how they work.

- Trace conditional expressions, for example, if statements and macros, which assert on the value you are analyzing, especially when they yield errors and panics. This is a clear indication something will go wrong under specific conditions.

195

- For values which represent minimum, maximum, etc. – inspect your current on-chain data to see whether you have outliers. For example, if I am about to reconfigure a setting related to minimum amount, do I already have on-chain participants which are staking less than the proposed new amount? Sort of a boundary-value analysis against the existing data.

- These "specific conditions" become the prerequisites before you can apply migrations and update the setting to its newly desired value. That's the start of testing this area further.

The above list is just a rough outline. It is important to note that it must be codified into a more formal process for engineers and stakeholders to follow with several places in this process where we can stop, evaluate pros and cons, and make decisions. Another important item is that such process and evaluation must not take too long, or at least be predictable so that you can deliver software changes in a timely manner. And that is the bane of all software development and testing – how do you estimate the unknown and how do you manage risk when you have no idea how all of the little pieces are supposed to work and when there are thousands of little pieces that you rely upon?

Resource Management for Testing in Production Environments

I've already mentioned how I am capable of testing against multiple environments and whenever possible would also like to exercise test suites against a production environment, including test suites for any third-party components. The challenge then becomes how do you clean up after yourself when you have long periods of time between steps, see Figure 7-7?

CHAPTER 7   CREDITCOIN 3.0

Any operation related to staking will need to be followed by an unbond transaction eventually, then waiting for a downtime period and then withdrawal of funds. In certain scenarios there may be more steps, more actors, and more waiting involved. The period is based on block time and number of eras, for example, one validation cycle. When doing all of this locally or in CI, it is relatively quick, and you also have full control over all values and the environment. When doing the same in production, the difference is drastic – era time is 24 hours. Unbonding period is 7 days. Certain operations also depend on when exactly during these 24 hours you issue the transaction leading to even more wait time. It's a rolling window of time which can take anywhere between 12 and 36 hours for the effect to take place.

Obviously you cannot have your test suite running for 7 days and waiting to clean up after itself – that is just a waste of resources. You can split it up and say execute the cleanup portion separately via cron – this opens up the question of storing and sharing credentials between test suites/cleanup tools.

This also brings the question of how to assert on long running tasks which are straightforward to automate? For example, becoming a validator on the Creditcoin blockchain is a relatively easy process; there is even the `wizard` command in the cli which performs all steps for you. However this command only signals an intention. The results do not take effect immediately. It can take anywhere between 12 and 36 hours, assuming everything else is good for a participant to become an active validator after they signal their intentions and the respective transactions make it into a block.

How do you assert that whatever the testsuite did actually result in the expected outcome? How do you make sure that dynamically provisioned resources, for example, a virtual machine or a container, do not get recycled before they are actually needed or are not left dangling afterward?

One possibility here is only manual testing disregarding the fact that you spent time to automate your test suite. Another possibility is a tiered approach where all functionality will be tested in isolation and only partially tested against production environments. This opens up the question of confidence.

A third possibility, depicted in Figure 7-8, is to split the traditional *setup-act-assert-teardown* flow into multiple stand-alone pieces which could be executed independently, for example, via cron or some sort of a queue. These independent automation parts will need to share data between themselves, and probably the easiest way, in the context of testing a blockchain, is to record such data on-chain directly – no need for an extra SQL database. QA and stakeholders should be able to query this data for the purposes of status reports. However, this doesn't solve the problem of triggering these automated scripts – smart contracts cannot initiate actions on their own, so you need an external process to call a function from the smart contract every so often. Very long running functions inside a smart contract also face the challenge that they will run out of gas and be reverted so you can't call a function at the beginning of your test; have it sleep for a few days and then let it clean up. It is also not possible for smart contracts to interface with the off-chain world and call API functions across the Internet, for example. There are available solutions like ChainAPI, `https://chainapi.com/`, which I haven't tried yet.

I think a practical solution for orchestration of long-running testing scenarios here would look something like this:

- Trigger tests *setup* + *act* scripts.

- Testing state data gets recorded in a shared location, possibly on-chain via a smart contract.

- Automated scripts that should be executed in the future are recorded in a queue, possibly with an estimated block number when they need to be executed.

- At a future time the *assert + teardown* parts are executed; the results recorded back on-chain via the smart contract.

- In certain situations the *teardown* part itself is a long running task with multiple steps. For example, unbond funds, and then withdraw them after a week. Follow the already described process for this as well.

In the context of having access to a blockchain, and testing the same blockchain, I believe it makes sense to just record shared data onto the chain itself as yet another way of eating your own dog food. However, that isn't strictly necessary. You could use a standard SQL database and build your own reports or better yet use a test management system like the open source Kiwi TCMS which already has the necessary functionality built-in.

Disclaimer I am the project lead of Kiwi TCMS too!

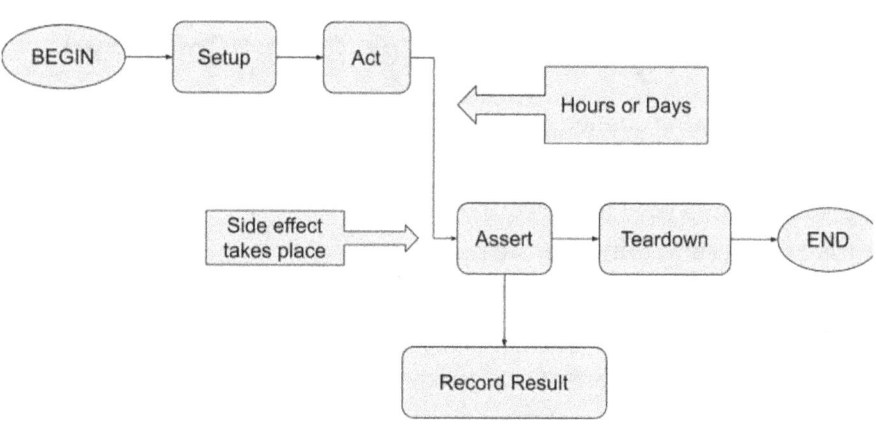

Figure 7-7. *Illustration of where a traditional testing sequence breaks before long-running processes in a blockchain kick into effect*

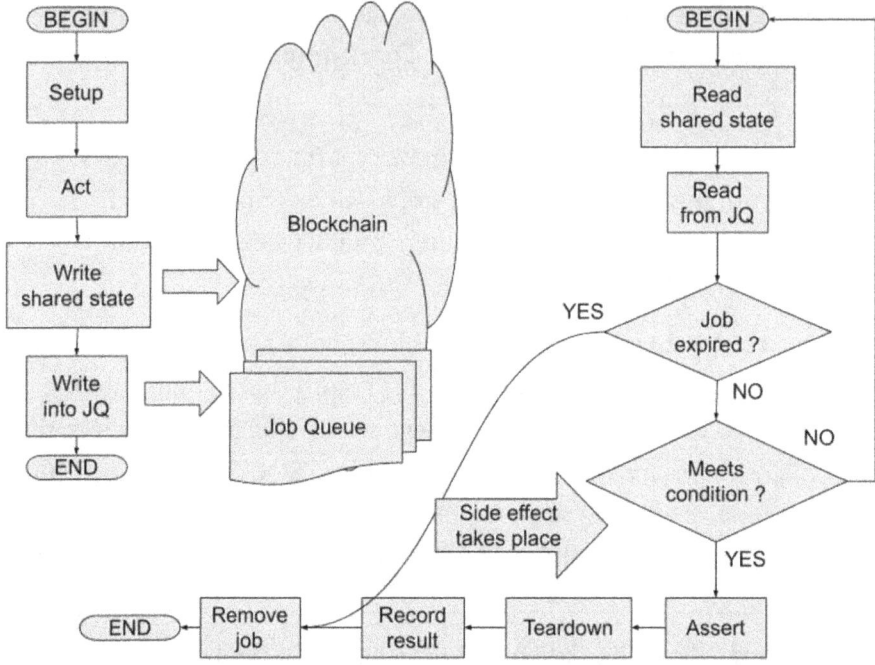

Figure 7-8. *Schematic depiction of the proposed test orchestrator*

Troubleshooting Guides and Sos-Report Command

Another interesting challenge I've come across has to do with community interactions. For whatever reasons somebody will end up having troubles – either they didn't read the documentation, or didn't pay enough attention or tried doing something that was never expected – users are good at this, perhaps even better than us testers. It could be the case that there has genuinely been some sort of a technical problem at the time when the user was trying to perform an operation or that the user wasn't tech savvy enough to understand the documentation or that they simply made a mistake. When that happens, they will reach out to available communication and support channels and complain about their problem.

CHAPTER 7   CREDITCOIN 3.0

Because of everything that happens in a blockchain, the long periods involved and also because your user base isn't necessarily technical, the initial problem report will always be missing important information. Sometimes it will be easier for engineering to guess what the actual problem was and offer a solution to be communicated back; other times it may be entirely impossible. To be clear this is much more likely to happen in the event someone wants to become an active validator rather than trying to become a nominator via the Creditcoin Staking Dashboard.

To combat this situation, I am proposing a two-step approach:

1. Curating a list of common questions and requests for additional information – this is to make sure you can collect as much initial data from the user as possible and also cover commonly known pitfalls and edge cases. Whenever the user contacts your support team, they will be asked to provide answers to these questions. The sooner this happens the better – for example, if a user shuts off their computer and then retries on the next morning, chain-state will have changed so their actions may result in a slightly different outcome. Ideally this list of questions is publicly available in the documentation, and users are aware what sort of information they should provide when contacting support.

2. Logs, local results, computer uptime, process uptime, and many other data are actually possible to be queried directly from the blockchain and the host running a creditcoin3-node process. Listing open ports, trying to reach out well-known Creditcoin URLs across the Internet, measuring networking speed, etc. are also possible. I call this

201

the `sos-report` command similar to something I've seen in commercial Linux distributions. Ideally this command will be part of the docker container, will collect all of the necessary information from step 1, and then allow the user to review it and submit it to the support team!

This proposal is also where you start building your knowledge base and expanding the support services offered to the public. While not strictly a testing-related activity, it can benefit overall quality in a few ways.

- Testers can learn a lot from the actual users on the field – this is real-world usage of the software under test, and we can use this knowledge to improve test coverage where needed.

- In the event of known issues, testers are likely to have already seen it or to be familiar with the issue because we've got a lot of edge-case knowledge about the application collected through countless tests and exercising the same application. We can unlock this knowledge and share it with the rest of the organization.

Integration Tests Speed-Up

I've mentioned previously that the biggest part of the test suite for Creditcoin 3 is the CLI integration test suite. It contains the highest number of individual test scenarios and takes the most time to execute. On a per CI job basis, this execution time has grown to around 90 minutes for the longest jobs. While writing this book, I worked on a number of tasks to try and bring this down which of course starts by measuring how much testing do we actually do.

At the time of writing this book, there were over 7000 workflow runs in GitHub Actions for the gluwa/creditcoin3 repository alone. Of them CLI integration test jobs average roughly 1000 hours per month.

The initial speed-up targeted a few low hanging fruits:

- Reduce the value for hard-coded sleep calls, and remove such calls where possible.

- Rewrite setup sections so that related test scenarios would share their setup instead of each scenario having their own. That was especially useful for long running test scenarios like withdrawUnbonded.test.ts which need to wait 15+ minutes for the correct pre-conditions before they can actually do anything.

- Conditionally skip other long-running test scenarios, like validatorCycle.test.ts on purpose. This scenario takes around 20 minutes, with a maximum timeout of around 30 minutes, and acts like an end-to-end testing with all of the individual commands used inside of it tested separately in isolation. We don't need to repeat this on every single pull request, so I've added a conditional statement which will execute this scenario only on commits directly into the dev branch, for example, post merge. It is still executed on pull requests against other branches for extra safety before a new release.

The most significant change in this optimization space is switching away from GitHub's hosted runners onto self-hosted ones. This is something that I already use as part of runtime-upgrade testing so it was just a matter of adding a bit of extra configuration to the existing CI pipeline. In particular, provide self-hosted runners using a matrix job with the similar arguments as the integration-test-cli matrix. Label the newly provisioned runners with their respective labels according to the test matrix, and then use the same labels in the integration-test-cli job definition to select the appropriate runner. That guarantees six unique runners each one of which will be assigned to only one integration test job. Then destroy them when finished!

This effort lead to shaving off 30 minutes from the longest running test jobs in this matrix. My speculation is that even though there is a lot of waiting for blockchain-related operations, using these self-hosted runners is still faster than GitHub shared runners because they are a dedicated resource which isn't oversubscribed. I/O and most likely CPU operations will take less time because the underlying operating system is giving its full attention to your testing instead of juggling hundreds or thousands of other processes. I don't have a definitive proof if that's the actual reason, but it does make sense, and empirical results show that using these self-hosted runners is faster than using the shared ones!

Caution   Besides the limits of how many virtual machines you can provision at the same time in your hosting environment, there is another more subtle factor which may be imposing unexpected limitations on your CI. This is the API request limit rates set by your chosen cloud provider in relation to how often you need to provision resources on-demand. With Creditcoin 3 I've seen the underlying provisioning API respond with *429 Too Many Requests* often enough to be annoying and cause my CI setup failing!

This also tells me that the overall number of virtual machines that I can have at any given time has nothing to do with the number of how many API requests I am allowed per hour/per minutes, etc. This is something that needs to be evaluated in more details if your testing depends heavily on self-hosted runners.

CHAPTER 7   CREDITCOIN 3.0

All of this isn't very difficult to do with the existing syntax in GitHub Actions; however, it brings an unwanted side effect – you now have a matrix test job which depends on another matrix test job, see Figure 7-9. If one of the integration test jobs fails, or times out, there is no easy way to restart it. I mean you could click the restart button in the GitHub interface for that specific job which has failed, but it will lead to unwanted results. The best you can do is restart all jobs part of the matrix together – and that's simply not possible via the current GitHub interface – you have to restart all jobs defined in the same yaml file.

At the time of writing this book, this was a fairly recent problem, but I think I know what the solution should be. If there is one more CI job, before the *deploy-github-runner* one, that is, to the left of the dependency chain, it could serve as the entrypoint. Let's call it *integration-test-cli-entrypoint*. If any of the subsequent jobs needs to be restarted, a tester could restart the *integration-test-cli-entrypoint* job and everything else that comes after it. Still not very optimal, but it doesn't trigger a restart for every other CI job defined in the same yaml file. I'm definitely trying this out!

Figure 7-9. Dependent matrix jobs

205

CHAPTER 7   CREDITCOIN 3.0

Summary

As you have seen by now, testing Creditcoin 3 is very similar to its predecessors from the v2 family. That is to be expected because the underlying technology stack and development practices are roughly the same. On the other hand, there are new testing challenges that came up which I guess is also to be expected.

Unfortunately there is no more testing that I can share for now. As I am writing the book, the next phase of Creditcoin 3 is not there yet, and I haven't worked on it, not am I aware of the practical details related to its implementation.

In the next chapter, I will talk about how I approach testing in general and what I think a test engineer's job is. Please stick around a bit more.

PART IV

Blockchain Testing Approaches

CHAPTER 8

How Others Test Blockchain

My motivation for writing this book was to share my personal experience in blockchain testing in the hope that it could be useful to others. During the process of writing it, I actually came to know other testers who were working in the blockchain domain. And of course they were working on products which are different than mine, and their approach is also different.

This chapter outlines the experience of Andrew Snaith and Sebastian Viquez who kindly agreed to talk to me. As you will see, there is even more to test in blockchain than I have already covered in all the previous chapters.

My Blockchain Testing Approach

As with any other kind of testing, I start by trying to understand what we're trying to do and the limitations of the environment I am working in:

- What are all of the components of the blockchain under test?

- How does each component work, and what is its complexity?

CHAPTER 8   HOW OTHERS TEST BLOCKCHAIN

- What are the risks involved; what are the business requirements?
- What parts can be exercised via unit, integration, and/or other types of testing?
- How do I actually write these types of tests – for example, available tools, syntax, and examples?

This helps me build up my understanding of all moving parts from business point of view and also from a technical point of view. I tend to start from the technical side first and then gradually expand my understanding. Whenever possible, I will opt-in for testing early in the development cycle and automating as much as possible. That also helps to codify the behavior of a complex system which has been handy on numerous occasions.

For Creditcoin that means I was focusing mainly on testing business logic and covering additional scenarios as they arise and as we gain more understanding of how the entire blockchain is used and how it works in detail. Constantly participating in code review on pull requests, raising questions and opening tickets for missing tests or the need for refactoring so that they aren't forgotten has contributed more for quality over time than any particular test scenario I've automated or any individual bug I've found.

This is a bottom-up approach and is also a very organic one – testing from day one and testing every minimal bit of product that you can lay your hands on. This is also a personal bias that I have because of how my professional career has taken place over the years – I've always worked in product companies, always on products which are highly technical in nature and always on the same level as my developer counterparts. That is the nature of infrastructure-type software products anyway.

I'm not sure if I am even qualified to offer advice for anyone else not being in the same situation as I am in. I guess just "give it a try" is good enough advice.

CHAPTER 8   HOW OTHERS TEST BLOCKCHAIN

Testing Across the Blockchain Stack with Andrew Snaith

Testing a blockchain protocol and client implementation is one side of the puzzle and arguably the fact that Gluwa, Inc. controls both makes testing Creditcoin relatively easy. I talked to Andrew Snaith, Quality Engineering Lead at ChainSafe, about his point of view around blockchain testing and discovered even more nuances than I had previously thought about.

ChainSafe is a multi-chain blockchain research and development company with a focus on open source software. They offer development services for external clients and also develop their own products.

In terms of organization, the company has multiple engineering teams which for the majority part work on what they call streams. Some engineers are dedicated to a single stream, while others are working on multiple streams in parallel. Similarly some teams have a dedicated quality engineer, while others do not, more on this later. The work itself is spanning across multiple chains as well as across the entire stack: host client development, cross-chain bridges, web3 tooling libraries and SDKs, distributed applications, smart contracts, and browser extensions.

Note   A **bridge** is a computer program that connects two or more blockchains together usually for the purposes of transferring assets between them. Different chains are not natively connected to one another, so the bridge must make sure that token ownership and quantities are represented correctly in a cross-chain transfer.

> **Note** **Filecoin** is a decentralized blockchain-based storage network. It was developed by Protocol Labs[1] and shares some ideas from InterPlanetary File System[2] allowing users to rent unused disk space. The blockchain is based on both proof-of-replication and proof-of-spacetime[3] consensus algorithms.

Products Under Test

I'm not going to list every single project that ChainSafe works on, but here's a list of several notable products under test grouped in their respective categories. Please try to keep in mind this diversity because it reflects on how testing is performed.

Protocol Clients and Bridges

Lodestar[4] is an implementation of Ethereum consensus in the TypeScript language. It is a light client for Ethereum and is considered to be production grade.

Forest[5] is an alternative implementation of the Filecoin host client, written in the Rust programming language, while the official Filecoin client and reference implementation is written in the Go language. Forest is already considered to be in production.

---

[1] https://en.wikipedia.org/wiki/Protocol_Labs
[2] https://en.wikipedia.org/wiki/InterPlanetary_File_System
[3] https://en.wikipedia.org/wiki/Proof_of_space-time
[4] https://github.com/ChainSafe/lodestar
[5] https://github.com/ChainSafe/forest

Gossamer[6] is an implementation of the Polkadot host client written in Go which is not yet launched in production. This work is funded by the Polkadot Treasury after a successful Open Gov proposal.

It is important to note that all of these are essentially a third-party implementation of somebody else's open source protocol, while in the rest of this book I talk about protocol (the Creditcoin loan cycle and data structures) and client implementation (creditcoin-node) created by the same team! An important reason for client diversity is enhancing ecosystem security, that is, to prevent an attacker from exploiting bugs which may not exist in an alternative implementation. Here I mean bugs present in the client program itself, for example, logical errors, or bugs inherent to the programming language it was written in.

Sygma[7] is a modular, open source, cross-chain connectivity protocol which allows applications to interoperate across EVM, Substrate, and other chains. You can also see this referred to as a cross-chain bridge, for example, a software component that makes it possible to connect events across different blockchains. The exact scope of this components varies depending on business and functional needs.

Libraries and SDK

web3.js[8] – a very popular JavaScript library for building on Ethereum, an alternative to *ethers.js* which I've used. ChainSafe is the current maintainer of this open source library.

web3.unity[9] – an SDK for the Unity framework which allows games to interact with blockchains and provides an admin panel.

---

[6] https://github.com/ChainSafe/gossamer
[7] https://github.com/sygmaprotocol
[8] https://web3js.org/
[9] https://github.com/ChainSafe/web3.unity

You can find several more libraries on the ChainSafe GitHub page: https://github.com/orgs/ChainSafe/repositories?q=web3.

ChainSafe is also very proud of their *cypress-polkadot-wallet* plugin; however, this is not a core product but rather one of their testing tools so more on it a bit later.

Browser Extensions and Distributed Applications

Polkadot Wallet Snap for MetaMask[10] is a MetaMask plugin for interacting with distributed apps on Polkadot and other Substrate-based chains because a vanilla MetaMask installation can only work with Ethereum compatible chains.

Multix[11] is an interface to easily manage complex multi-signature wallets on the Polkadot blockchain.

Testing Strategy

Andrew, like myself, is coming into the blockchain world from a traditional software development and testing background. His value proposition is to bring his existing expertise into the blockchain domain. In practical terms, this means to balance the need for blockchain development to be nimble and fast yet at the same time define some processes like collecting product requirements, establishing a process of reviewing pull requests, creating test plans and executing them, adding test automation, and so on.

While my original impression was that there aren't many test engineers in blockchain because of the inherent complexity of distributed systems and also the relatively unfamiliar programming languages, Andrew brings a slightly different point of view:

---

[10] https://github.com/ChainSafe/metamask-snap-polkadot
[11] https://github.com/ChainSafe/Multix

- Blockchain development is still a pretty niche area in the world of software development. It's mostly made up of smaller teams and the technology stack is still new, so it can be tricky to find talent in general and testers in particular.

- Partly because of the immutability aspect, and I also think partly because of the nature of distributed systems, blockchain developers seem to have a higher level of testing experience compared to other domains in the IT industry. Or probably they are just more experienced developers because they need to be in order to work in this domain space.

- In terms of test writing at the unit and integration layer we see a lot; however, this is done by developers as one of many other responsibilities and is not a dedicated effort.

- Having someone who's really focused on quality process and risk mitigation is super important as building a high-quality product is much more than just test creation and test execution.

I will also add that some blockchain-related startups have been working on speculative coins and were under pressure to cut corners and seek fast exit rather than follow a traditional software development process and build a quality product. In this respect, Andrew is grateful not to have this challenge and aspect at ChainSafe.

CHAPTER 8   HOW OTHERS TEST BLOCKCHAIN

Due to the diversity of projects and teams at ChainSafe, and also in general, everyone's definition of what "high quality" means is different. Andrew is going with a practical model following the ISO 25010[12] standard – high quality is the level to which the software under test satisfied the requirements posted by its stakeholders. This generic model is used as a guideline principle at ChainSafe which then evolves according to the product and blockchain-specific needs.

According to Andrew, the challenges in terms of working with a blockchain are as follows:

- **Data immutability**: Blockchain state cannot be changed after it is recorded, and if your testing requires specific on-chain state, you can mitigate this by either using fresh testing accounts every time and/or using local and shared testnet chains. In Creditcoin I actually use fresh testing accounts most of the time coupled with the fact that the test suite does not depend on the actual data itself – just that it is present! I am probably missing some test coverage here.

- **Finality**: This is the level of confidence that a recently appended block will not be removed from the chain. The challenge here is that there are multiple nodes which operate independently from one another, and it is entirely possible that your transactions make it into a block on a specific node A at the same time in which another node B produces a block. This is what we call forking, and a healthy blockchain will be able to resolve these forks and eventually all nodes will be consistent with one another. The challenge for development and

---

[12] www.iso.org/standard/78176.html

CHAPTER 8   HOW OTHERS TEST BLOCKCHAIN

testing, especially for products like a bridge, is that when you examine the on-chain state, you may be looking at a fork of the canonical chain which would later be reverted, that is, it is not completely finalized yet. One way to resolve this is to wait for a certain amount of blocks, for example, 12, and then perform the assertions against the latest block. How much this grace period will be is usually based on your intimate knowledge of the underlying blockchain. This is also more likely to be a challenge when working with cross-chain applications rather than when working on a single chain.

- **Latency**: The delay between cause and effect in the system under test is a challenge which isn't specific to blockchain, but according to Andrew it is more of a factor in blockchain testing scenarios. For some projects, ChainSafe deals with this by deploying their release candidate clients into shared environments, for example, Testnet, and then records performance stats in Grafana for a specific period, usually 2 weeks. You can think of this as a soak test. At the end of the soak period, the current baseline is compared against previous releases and/or baselines from rival host clients and/or stakeholder requirements.

- **Data retention/data availability**: This refers to the fact that historical blockchain and off-chain data may no longer be available if node operators are not incentivized to keep it around. This becomes even more important in the context of NFTs because in many chains an NFT is just an on-chain receipt pointing to an external URL. This external resource

217

could be removed at any point. Contrast this with the NFT implementation on the *Sui* network,[13] where all data can be, but doesn't necessarily have to be, stored on-chain indefinitely. One way around this is to use pinning services such as *Pinata*[14] where you pay for your data to be persisted for a certain period of time. This is essentially a data mirroring service which guarantees availability of IPFS files. Another possible way around this is to operate the data mirroring service yourself and/or a so-called full node, which may be less cost effective when working on a third-party chain. When testing against public blockchain networks, you may hit a situation where expected data is missing which will cause the test suite to fail.

Squads with Dedicated QA Engineer

Certain teams at ChainSafe have a dedicated QA engineer who is assigned to the team full time. These engineers take part in all team activities such as standup meetings and pull request review. Their focus and the bulk of their testing happens on the pull request itself, before a new feature or a new change gets merged. Other testing activities are as follows:

- Supplementary testing in stand-alone environments, for example, stand-alone chains or testnet(s).

- Join early planning phase – review product requirement document(s) and discuss implementation details/raise questions with developers before any code gets written.

---

[13] https://blog.sui.io/onchain-storage-explained/
[14] www.pinata.cloud

- Work on test automation, primarily integration type testing, for new functionality.

Long-term goal here is for QA to become stronger and more valuable by constantly taking part in the development process.

Squads Without Dedicated QA Engineer

These are teams who are working on new projects, maybe on a proof of concept, etc. They consist predominantly from developers and mainly rely on unit and integration-type tests. The majority of these test suites are initially created by the developers themselves with QA engineers joining to fill in the gaps with the bulk of the testing being integration-type testing owned by the dev team. In such teams, QA engineers help and advise with testing-related activities, for example, creating test plans and test cases where needed or performing manual test execution but do not own the testing effort completely.

Here, depending on the product, the team may have a manual smoke test suite, and test engineers are expected to engage in user acceptance testing, end-to-end testing, and testing inside Testnet environments and/or automation tasks mostly happening outside of the git repository.

For example, when testing the *Sygma* bridge, there may be multiple steps which are executed against two different chains. In this situation QA engineers are more likely to work on some helper scripts that automate setting up the on-chain state and then perform verification and inspection manually, especially for new functionality and new integrations. This is a semi-automated testing approach rather than hacking on a full end-to-end test case. In the context of Creditcoin staking, I have previously described how a fully automated e2e test suite experiences challenges in cleaning up after itself due to having to wait too long for certain conditions to materialize on-chain. By not going 100% automated ChainSafe is able to avoid such issues.

CHAPTER 8   HOW OTHERS TEST BLOCKCHAIN

On Test Automation and Tools

Given the diverse nature of products and their stages of maturity, there isn't a one-size-fits-all requirement for test automation and code coverage metrics at ChainSafe. During the period in which a product is undergoing rapid iteration and proof-of-concept, there is usually not much investment in test automation. Teams are more likely to wait until the architecture model has been stabilized before starting to work on adding test automation and enabling CI jobs on pull requests in GitHub. This usually happens while new functionality is being added to the product under test.

In terms of programming languages and testing frameworks, ChainSafe teams are using the defaults coming from the language when it comes to unit and integration-type testing in the same repository which ranges between Go, Rust, and TypeScript. The rule of thumb for Andrew is "use the standard testing tools built into the language." This is what he also calls "core-testing."

As we go up the testing pyramid into e2e and UAT testing, the tools become a bit more standardized with a clear preference to use Cypress for anything that touches a user interface. Using Cypress however hits limitations when you have to interact with browser extensions that sign and submit transactions to the underlying blockchain – it isn't directly supported, although there are workarounds and third-party plugins; see `https://github.com/cypress-io/cypress/issues/16703` and `https://github.com/cypress-io/cypress/issues/14808`. Hacking Cypress to speak to a browser extension is possible; however, ChainSafe prefers not to add that complexity into their testing tools as they lose the ability for introspection when sending commands from Cypress to the extension and the ability to listen to blockchain events which may not be reported/observable through the DOM or rather may not be observable through the extension itself.

For the situation in which the subject under test is a distributed application, but not the wallet extension itself, Andrew's primary goal is to guarantee the functionality of the dApp under test that's why he prefers to remove the wallet from the picture entirely. Essentially creating a false, programmatically controlled wallet, inside the test suite itself by stubbing out the `window.ethereum` object, for example, mocking the EVM side. The assumption is that the extension works as expected, and it doesn't need to be tested explicitly. In practice browser extensions are still subjected to testing, at the very least via a manual smoke test, because you still need to know that the distributed application and the extension work well together and there are no obvious issues, or document them if there are.

This approach didn't work well for *Multix* because wallets work slightly differently for Polkadot than for Ethereum-based chains. Also because for a multisig wallet, Andrew discovered that they need to workaround more scenarios. The solution here is a programmable wallet library that connects your test framework to the Polkadot API. This is the previously mentioned *cypress-polkadot-wallet* plugin which can be found at `https://github.com/chainsafe/cypress-polkadot-wallet`.

On the other hand, if you don't have the resources to create your own testing tools and libraries and/or the ones by ChainSafe don't fit your use case, you may go ahead with Playwright for UI test automation. I have seen a working test suite exercising several browser extensions, using the Chrome browser, which can sign and submit transactions. May not be very elegant but is a relatively easy way to get started.

Other tools used by ChainSafe:

- Chopsticks, `https://github.com/AcalaNetwork/chopsticks`, is a forking tool for Substrate-based networks similar to our own creditcoin-fork.

- Dappeteer, `https://github.com/ChainSafe/dappeteer`, now archived, is a library to facilitate end-to-end testing for dApps using Puppeteer + MetaMask. This was created originally by ChainSafe for signing dapps under test with a real metamask extension but later utilized further for testing their snaps development work within MetaMask.

For smart contracts, testing activities revolve around logic verification, vulnerabilities scanning, and security audits, including from external third-party providers.

Testing Smart Contracts with Sebastian Viquez

During my journey of testing Creditcoin, I have worked predominantly on testing at the protocol layer itself and almost not at the layer that sits on top of it – that is a blockchain application implemented as a smart contract. I even mentioned in the beginning of this book that practical applications of smart contracts are outside of the scope of this book.

Well, well, well. Given that Creditcoin has now evolved into a general purpose blockchain which supports smart contracts, it is only fitting that we actually get to hear a different point of view from someone with more experience in this area.

I talked to Sebastian Viquez, a fellow QA lead and an early Bitcoin adopter from Costa Rica. What follows is a summary of his experience.

Note A smart contract is a computing program that is recorded onto the blockchain itself! It can store data on-chain, execute other smart contract programs, and emit events. Users interact with smart contracts by sending transactions to the address on which the smart contract is deployed. From a user point of view, these interactions are performed via a wallet application such as MetaMask.

Product Under Test

For the purposes of this book, we are going to refer to the application under test with a madeup name: *The NFT Marketplace*. Note that the name and description is made up; however, the core product functionality isn't.

Tip **Non-fungible tokens** or **NFTs** are unique digital assets, recorded onto a blockchain, that come with cryptographically verifiable ownership. The metadata of NFTs makes them unique, which means no two NFTs can ever be the same. This metadata can be linked to digital files, for example. You can think about an **NFT** as an identifier or a receipt which can be used to certify proof of ownership and authenticity. The term *non-fungible* means that it is unique and cannot be replaced with something else; in other words, each token is very specific. On the other end are regular cryptocurrency tokens which are fungible, that is, they are similar to one another and can be easily exchanged.

NFTs are created via a process called minting which also involves interacting with a smart contract. The main objective of minting an NFT is to get your digital content onto the blockchain while proving

CHAPTER 8 HOW OTHERS TEST BLOCKCHAIN

ownership of your digital art or item. Depending on the actual blockchain, the digital art which the NFT points to may use on-chain or off-chain storage!

Smart contracts implementing NFTs follow standards which are already established in the blockchain ecosystem, for example, ERC-721 and ERC-1155. In contrast, popular crypto tokens follow another standard, for example, ERC-20. More about these standards can be found at https://vegavid.com/blog/erc20-vs-erc721-vs-erc1155/#.

Digital content can be endlessly copied, and there is no way to tell one file apart from another, that is, there is no distinction between an original and a copy. Using an NFT's unique identifier helps distinguish one NFT from another – that is, distinguish one digital file from another, even if their contents are the same. This in turn opens up more possibilities for creators in the digital world looking to profit from their work.

The NFT Marketplace is an application which allows its users to transact with NFT assets representing images based on their subscription level. Users can view, buy, sell, or auction different digital assets. They can also gain value points and monitor how their assets are increasing in value based on interactions from other users, for example, how many likes their images have.

The NFT Marketplace application is comprised of a traditional Web 2.0 front-end, a minting process, and a collection of several smart contracts which

- Manage user accounts where multiple roles are defined: *regular user, admin, artist*. Each role permits a different set of functionalities.

- The NFTs minting process which involves creating a digital item or file, designing the artwork to accompany the item, establishing a text file with code, uploading the file to an NFT smart contract, and publishing it on the NFT marketplace.

- Handle asset transactions, for example, transfers to other users. In the minting process, smart contracts are used to assign ownership and handle the transfer of the NFT while proving the item's authenticity. When a piece of art is minted as an NFT, it is assigned a unique identifier directly linked to a single blockchain address. Each digital art has an owner, and the ownership details are publicly available on the blockchain and can be verified. Even if a creator mints 1,000 NFTs of the same item, each one of them can easily be distinguished from the rest by its unique identifier.

- Implement the marketplace and related application functionality. Imagine a website where you can upload an image and convert this image into a digital asset to include it in your profile account as an artist would when showing all of their paintings to sell in a showroom. It's the same concept, but adding other factors, such as social media likes and site views, the more people like it, the more value acquired, the more money an artist could make.

The application is deployed on the Polygon blockchain network and its main objectives are

1. To encourage users to be part of the subscription based on the assets which they can mint, acquire, sell or transfer

Chapter 8   How Others Test Blockchain

2. To increase value of the available assets in the marketplace using subscriptions and minting fees

Users are able to exchange their NFTs by using a wallet application, which in this example is MetaMask.

Testing

Sebastian has described his testing strategy into a Medium.com article, https://medium.com/@sebas.viquez/simple-test-strategy-for-web3-apps-using-hardhat-testing-framework-2e5efa21e98e, and I urge you to read it in details. Here's the gist of it:

- Start with unit testing smart contracts, using the popular Hardhat tool in order to verify the correctness of each individual function inside your smart contract(s). You can configure Hardhat to use its own embedded Ethereum chain, another local chain like Ganache, or an external chain like Goerli (a named Ethereum Testnet instance).

- Then move onto integration testing in order to exercise different parts of the Web3 application. In particular focusing on interactions between multiple smart contracts.

- Moving onto security-related testing with tools like MythX[15], or Slither[16], to analyze your smart contracts for common security vulnerabilities. Given these are more like static analysis tools, I personally would move them toward the bottom of the testing pyramid and include them very early into the process.

---

[15] https://mythx.io/
[16] https://www.alchemy.com/dapps/slither

CHAPTER 8   HOW OTHERS TEST BLOCKCHAIN

- End-to-end testing which also includes the user interface for the application. For the UI portion of the tests, use your favorite tool. An interesting piece here is the truffle-assertions[17] library which allows tests to assert on events emitted by smart contracts.

- What Sebastian calls *"Blockchain Network Testing"* is actually deploying your contracts to a blockchain network running in the real world, rather than using a chain locally on your computer, and then exercising the application and the test suite again. Due to the cost of tokens on a real chain, a testnet like environment, for example, Goerli and Sepolia, can be used before moving to mainnet. Inevitably that leads to the test suite having to execute some scenarios conditionally. This approach is also something that I like to do quite a lot as described in earlier chapters in this book. The most certain way to know whether the application will work in real life is to execute as much as you can in production.

- Sebastian describes load and performance testing using the k6[18] tool; however, any tool that you are familiar with should work here. On the other hand, my personal approach for performance and load testing has been to interact with the blockchain directly, sending transactions using a chain-specific client library.

---

[17] https://archive.trufflesuite.com/
[18] https://k6.io

CHAPTER 8   HOW OTHERS TEST BLOCKCHAIN

A notable testing challenge for *The NFT Marketplace* was the fact that your entrypoint for testing is a random address on a blockchain and not much else. One way to interact with the application and retrieve data is by using a client library, for example, *ethers.js*; another way is to extract the data and/or perform interactions using higher level tools such as Postman or the RestAssured library. This isn't something I am very keen on because I believe it represents more work on my side as a test engineer and because I also prefer to program rather than use one-size-fits-all type of tools; however, it is perfectly possible. Remember that in order for a blockchain network to be useful for external parties, it exports an API interface usually via standard RPC protocols, and this is where tools like Postman can plug into. Maybe that's more useful in the situation where you as a tester need to perform exploratory testing and need tools which allow you to interact with the blockchain manually. I've had limited similar experience due to the nature of my work, and it's hard for me to relate.

Another interesting challenge mentioned by Sebastian is knowing how much every operation in *The NFT Marketplace* costs and also to some extent being able to control that because transaction costs will have a direct impact on user experience and application adoption and the price of participating in a marketplace. Here Sebastian has made extensive use of the Ganache[19] tool, in order to easily simulate specific conditions before examining and testing *The NFT Marketplace*. You can think about Ganache as a tool which lets you to mock and control everything about the blockchain before testing the application that sits on top of it. This approach should make it possible for you as a tester to be able to understand all of the internals of your smart contracts under test even before deploying to a public blockchain.

---

[19] https://archive.trufflesuite.com/ganache/

A short demonstration video from testing this NFT marketplace application was previously available on LinkedIn. In it we could notice the following testing scenarios executed which give us a bit more insight into the functionality under test:

- Should transfer NFT and pay 250MATIC off market royalties
- Should not mint tokens if contract is paused
- Should not mint tokens if public mint locked
- Should not let users mint more than 5 NFTs
- Should mint more than max NFTs
- Should only allow admin to set token URI
- Should not pay royalties if in excludedList
- Should not transfer NFT if not enough token for royalties
- Should add/remove from excludedList
- Should transfer NFTs using market transfer method and award the artist 6% of sale amount

The code from the demonstration mentioned above is shown in Listing 8-1.

Listing 8-1. nft-test.js

```
const { expect } = require('chai');
const { ethers } = require('hardhat');

describe('NFT', async () => {
  let admin, artist, owner1, owner2;
```

CHAPTER 8   HOW OTHERS TEST BLOCKCHAIN

```javascript
  const offMarketTransferFee = ethers.utils.parseUnits("250",
  "ether");
  const mintPrice = ethers.utils.parseUnits("75", "ether");
  const maxNFTS = 10;

  let token, nft;

  beforeEach(async () => {
    ([admin, artist, owner1, owner2] = await ethers.
    getSigners());

    const Token = await ethers.getContractFactory('MockToken');
    token = await Token.deploy();
    await token.deployed();
    await token.transfer(
      owner1.address,
      ethers.utils.parseUnits("500", "ether")
    );

    await token.transfer(
      owner2.address,
      ethers.utils.parseUnits("500", "ether")
    );

    const NFT  = await ethers.getContractFactory('SNFT');
    nft = await NFT.deploy(artist.address, token.address, 6,
    offMarketTransferFee, mintPrice, maxNFTS);
    await nft.deployed();

    nft = nft.connect(admin)
    await nft.safeMint(artist.address, "0x");
  });

  it('Should transfer NFT and pay 250MATIC off market
  royalties', async () => {
```

```
  let ownerNFT, balanceSender, balanceArtist;

  nft = nft.connect(artist);
  await nft.transferFrom(
    artist.address,
    owner1.address,
    0
  );
  ownerNFT = await nft.ownerOf(0)
  expect(ownerNFT)
    .to
    .equal(owner1.address);

  await token.connect(owner1).approve(nft.address,
  offMarketTransferFee);
  await nft.connect(owner1).transferFrom(
    owner1.address,
    owner2.address,
    0
  );
  ownerNFT = await nft.ownerOf(0);
  balanceSender = await token.balanceOf(owner1.address);
  balanceArtist = await token.balanceOf(artist.address);
  expect(ownerNFT)
    .to
    .equal(owner2.address);
  expect(balanceSender.toString())
    .to
    .equal(ethers.utils.parseUnits('250', 'ether'));
  expect(balanceArtist.toString())
    .to
    .equal(ethers.utils.parseUnits('250', 'ether'));
});
```

CHAPTER 8   HOW OTHERS TEST BLOCKCHAIN

```javascript
it('Should not mint tokens if contract is paused',
async () => {
  // only admin role can pause contract
  nft = nft.connect(admin);
  await nft.pause();

  nft = nft.connect(owner1);
  await expect(nft.preMint(artist.address))
    .to.be.reverted;

  // make sure we can mint after unpausing
  nft = nft.connect(admin);
  await nft.unpause();
  await nft.grantMinterRole(owner1.address);

  nft = nft.connect(owner1);
  await token.connect(owner1).approve(nft.address,
  mintPrice);
  await nft.preMint();

  ownerNFT = await nft.ownerOf(1);
  expect(ownerNFT)
    .to
    .equal(owner1.address);
});

it('Should not mint tokens if public mint locked',
async () => {
  // only admin role can pause contract
  nft = nft.connect(admin);
  await nft.lockPublicMinting();

  nft = nft.connect(owner1);
  await expect(nft.mint())
    .to.be.reverted;
```

CHAPTER 8 HOW OTHERS TEST BLOCKCHAIN

```
  // make sure we can mint after unpausing
  nft = nft.connect(admin);
  await nft.unlockPublicMinting();

  nft = nft.connect(owner1);
  await token.connect(owner1).approve(nft.address,
  mintPrice);
  await nft.mint();

  ownerNFT = await nft.ownerOf(1);
  expect(ownerNFT)
    .to
    .equal(owner1.address);
});

it('Should not let users mint more than 5 NFTs',
async () => {
  // only admin role can pause contract
  nft = nft.connect(admin);
  await nft.grantMinterRole(owner1.address);

  nft = nft.connect(owner1);
  await token.connect(owner1).approve(nft.address, ethers.
  utils.parseUnits("500", "ether"));

  // mint 5 NFT's
  for(let i = 1; i <= 5; i++) {
    await nft.preMint();
    ownerNFT = await nft.ownerOf(i);
    expect(ownerNFT)
    .to
    .equal(owner1.address);
  }
```

```
    balanceArtist = await token.balanceOf(artist.address);

    // expect artist to have been paid 75MATIC for each mint
    expect(ethers.utils.formatEther(balanceArtist))
      .to
      .equal("375.0")

    // minting this 6 NFT should fail
    await expect(nft.preMint())
      .to.be.reverted;
  });

  it('Should mint more than max NFTS', async () => {
    // only admin role can pause contract
    nft = nft.connect(admin);
    await nft.grantMinterRole(owner1.address);

    nft = nft.connect(admin);

    // mint max 10 NFTs
    for(let i = 1; i <= 10; i++) {
      await nft.safeMint(admin.address, "0x");
    }

    // minting this 11 NFT should fail
    await expect(nft.safeMint(admin.address, "0x"))
      .to.be.reverted;
  });

  it('Should only allow admin to set token URI', async () => {
    // attempt to set token uri without admin role
        should revert
    nft = nft.connect(artist);

    const expectedTokenURI = "https://example.io/nft.json"
```

CHAPTER 8 HOW OTHERS TEST BLOCKCHAIN

```
    await expect(nft.setTokenURI(0, expectedTokenURI))
      .to.be.reverted;

    nft = nft.connect(admin);
    await nft.setTokenURI(0, expectedTokenURI);

    actualTokenURI = await nft.tokenURI(0);
    expect(actualTokenURI)
      .to
      .equal(expectedTokenURI)

    ownerNFT = await nft.ownerOf(0);
    expect(ownerNFT)
      .to
      .equal(artist.address);
});
it('Should not pay royalties if in excludedList',
async () => {
    let balanceSender, balanceArtist;

    nft =  nft.connect(artist);
    await nft.transferFrom(
      artist.address,
      owner1.address,
      0
    );
    balanceArtist = await token.balanceOf(artist.address);
    expect(balanceArtist)
      .to
      .equal(0);

    await nft.setExcluded(owner1.address, true);
    nft =  nft.connect(owner1);
```

235

CHAPTER 8 HOW OTHERS TEST BLOCKCHAIN

```
    await nft.transferFrom(
      owner1.address,
      owner2.address,
      0
    );
    balanceSender = await token.balanceOf(owner1.address);
    balanceArtist = await token.balanceOf(artist.address);
    expect(balanceSender)
      .to
      .equal(ethers.utils.parseUnits('500', 'ether'));
    expect(balanceArtist)
      .to
      .equal(0);
  });

  it('Should not transfer NFT if not enough token for
  royalties', async () => {
    nft = nft.connect(artist);
    await nft.transferFrom(
      artist.address,
      owner1.address,
      0
    );
    token = token.connect(owner1);
    await token.transfer(owner2.address, ethers.utils.
    parseUnits('500'));
    await token.approve(nft.address, offMarketTransferFee);
    nft = nft.connect(owner1);

    await expect(nft.transferFrom(owner1.address, owner2.
    address, 0))
```

CHAPTER 8   HOW OTHERS TEST BLOCKCHAIN

```
    .to.be.revertedWith('ERC20: transfer amount exceeds
    balance');
});

it('Should add/remove from excludedList', async () => {
  nft = nft.connect(artist);
  await nft.setExcluded(owner1.address, true);
  expect(await nft.excludedList(owner1.address))
    .to.equal(true);
  await nft.setExcluded(owner1.address, false);
  expect(await nft.excludedList(owner1.address))
    .to.equal(false);

  nft = nft.connect(owner2);
  await expect(nft.setExcluded(owner2.address, true))
    .to.be.revertedWith('artist only');
});

it('Should transfer NFT using market transfer method and
award the artist 6% of sale amount', async () => {
  nft = nft.connect(artist);
  await nft.transferFrom(
    artist.address,
    owner1.address,
    0
  );

  nft = nft.connect(owner1);
  token = token.connect(owner1);
  token.approve(nft.address, ethers.utils.parseUnits("100",
  "ether"))
```

237

CHAPTER 8   HOW OTHERS TEST BLOCKCHAIN

```
      const GiftMarketRoyaltyPercentage = await nft.
      GiftMarketRoyaltyPercentage()

      const offMarkeyRoyaltyAmount = await nft.
      offMarkeyRoyaltyAmount()

      console.log(GiftMarketRoyaltyPercentage.toString())
      console.log(offMarkeyRoyaltyAmount.toString())

      const amount = await nft.GiftMarketTransferFrom(owner1.
      address, owner2.address, 0, ethers.utils.parseUnits("100",
      "ether"))

      let balanceSender = await token.balanceOf(owner1.address);
      let balanceArtist = await token.balanceOf(artist.address);

      expect(balanceArtist.toString())
        .to
        .equal(ethers.utils.parseUnits("6", "ether"));

      ownerNFT = await nft.ownerOf(0)

      console.log(ethers.utils.formatEther(balanceSender),
      ethers.utils.formatEther(balanceArtist))
   });
});
```

Code summary:

- **Setup:** Contracts are deployed and initialized; testing accounts are initialized.

- **Transfer tests:** Ensure NFTs can be transferred and proper royalties are paid.

- **Minting tests:** Verify minting functionality under various conditions – paused contract, locked public minting, exceeding mint limits.

- **Admin functions:** Ensure only admins can perform certain actions, for example, setting token URI.

- **Exclusion list:** Test functionality related to excluding addresses from royalty payments.

- **Sufficient balance check:** Verify that NFT transfers only occur if the sender has sufficient tokens to cover royalties.

- **Market transfers:** Test specific market transfer methods and related royalties.

In a presentation titled *Blockchain Testing Frameworks Challenges* delivered few years ago at the TestWarez testing conference in Poland, Sebastian mentions multiple blockchain components and layers on which we can and should test, but I need to point out that this does not apply to everyone in every situation. I would argue that many blockchain-related applications focus only on certain layers of the stack, and this is where the majority of the testing will happen.

In the example described above, *The NFT Marketplace* is essentially a smart contract, and depending on the business requirements, there may not be a need to go testing further than that. A counterexample is Creditcoin, where the primary testing is on the protocol layer. Even though in Creditcoin 2.x we made a switch from proof-of-work to proof-of-stake consensus, we didn't test the algorithm implementation itself. We tested the transitioning procedure, the ability to preserve on-chain data and block history, but the consensus algorithm itself is a ready-made component which our implementation ingested, almost as a drop-in replacement.

CHAPTER 8   HOW OTHERS TEST BLOCKCHAIN

One quote from the presentation which I particularly like is

How to test a smart contract if we don't fully understand it and don't have the knowledge and tools to test it?

—Sebastian Viquez

Definitely agree with this and just replace the words *"smart contract"* with whatever blockchain component you happen to be working with. I have worked primarily on testing the data model and transactions layer which is relatively straightforward. Regardless it took me a long time to be able to fully understand all of the components involved and their internal interactions before I felt comfortable in my environment. If you as a tester are new to a project and new to blockchain technology, you are bound to go through the same experience.

On the tools spectrum, I was surprised to learn about *Hyperledger Caliper*[20], a performance benchmarking tool which I could have used during the Creditcoin 1.x time frame. Instead my team and I went for in-house tooling because that's what we knew how to do, and frankly I joined relatively late in the development cycle to have had any time to research and find this tool. During Creditcoin 2.x and then 3.0, my team performed more performance benchmarking, and this time around we were aware of existing tools for the Substrate ecosystem. However, we went for in-house solutions again because the existing tools were not immediately suitable for our use case, and it was just faster for us to create what we needed instead of figuring out how to workaround the limitations of a tool we had no experience with. This only goes to show that there are still areas in which the tooling and test framework ecosystem may not be mature enough or may not fit your particular testing needs.

---

[20] https://www.hyperledger.org/projects/caliper

Summary

As you have seen by now, blockchain testing can be very colorful. There are many areas in which we can test and also many tools that we can use. Despite that and despite the inherent complexity in certain software components, blockchain testing is not super different from traditional software testing.

Thank you for reading so far into this book. I hope that you have enjoyed it and learned something valuable that you can apply in your day-to-day work!

Happy testing!

Index

A
AddBidOrder, 8
Aella, 46
Airdrop, 15

B
Bitcoin, 3, 8, 10, 45, 60, 222
Blockchain attributes, 6
    fault tolerance, 7
    finality, 8
    permissionless *vs.* permissioned, 8
    public *vs.* private, 8
    reliability, 7
    reproducibility, 7
    security, 7
    testing requirements, 7
    transparency, 7
Blockchain components, 19
    block production, 22, 23
    block rewards, 22
    consensus algorithm, 19
    metrics and telemetry, 25
    migrations, 24
    off-chain worker/oracle, 25
    peer-to-peer networking, 19
    polygon network and its components, 18
    RPC API, 22, 23
    runtime upgrades, 24
    smart contracts, 25, 26
    storage, 23
    transaction fees, 21
    transactions, 20, 21
Blockchain development frameworks
    blockchain implementation, 35
    development and testing, 38–40
    Ethereum, 31
    Hyperledger Sawtooth, 29, 30
    programming languages, 31–34
    substrate, 30, 31
Blockchain implementations, 6, 7, 11, 16, 17, 22, 35–37, 49, 54, 81, 121, 149
Blockchain integration test suite, 172
Blockchain networks, 4, 7, 8, 11–15, 21, 25, 26, 28, 44, 45, 130, 225, 227, 228
Blockchain Network Testing, 227
Blockchain node, 13, 19, 23, 47, 90, 106

INDEX

Blockchain protocol, 8, 11, 211
Blockchains, 201, 210
    algorithms and software architecture, 6
    attributes (*see* Blockchain attributes)
    components (*see* Blockchain components)
    cryptographic functions, 6
    data availability, 217
    data immutability, 216
    data latency, 217
    data retention, 217
    finality, 216
    implementation, 6
    linked data blocks, 5
    as secure distributed ledger, 6
Blockchain stack
    products under test, 212
        browser extensions, 214
        distributed apps, 214
        libraries and SDK, 213, 214
        protocol clients and bridges, 212, 213
    testing strategy
        development, 215
        generic model, 216
        immutability aspect, 215
        processes, 214
        QA engineer, 218
        quality process/risk mitigation, 215
        semi-automated testing approach, 219
        test automation, 220–222
        test engineers, 219
        test suites, 219
        test writing, 215
        tools, 220–222
Blockchain technology, 3, 16, 35, 240
Blockchain testing, 3, 209–210, 217, 241
Blockchain transactions, 8
Block explorer, 9, 162
Block fullness, 10, 85, 122
Block hash, 10, 80, 132
Block height, 10, 24, 81
Block miners, 84
Block number, 10, 11, 80, 81, 127, 128, 151, 198
Block production, 21–22
Block rewards, 22
Block saturation, 10
Block time, 10–11, 26–28, 195, 197
Borderless Financial Platform, 43
Bottom-up approach, 210
Bridge, 163, 211–213
20-bytes, 14, 161
32-bytes, 14, 162

C

CAPTCHA test, 15
Cargo audit, 119
cargo test command, 91, 93
Cargo.toml, 192
ccclient, 55, 71

INDEX

ChainSafe, 211–222
Chopsticks, 221
Client program, 16, 24, 46, 213
Code coverage metric, 97, 137, 174
Code review, 39, 68, 70, 210
Coins, 13, 15, 123, 215
Consensus algorithm, 5, 12, 19, 58, 129, 159, 239
Consensus engine, 19, 26, 140
Consensus mechanism, 15, 26, 125
   PoA, 28
   PoS, 27
   PoW, 27
Credal, 46
Creditcoin 1.8, 62, 63, 72, 76
Creditcoin 1.x, 53, 55
   components
      client, 55, 56
      consensus, 57, 58
      Creditcoin-Legacy-Docker-Compose, 62
      Creditcoin-Legacy-Docker-Compose-Testnet, 62
      Creditcoin-Legacy-Tests, 61, 62
      gateway, 60
      REST API, 59, 60
      SDKs, 61
      transaction processors, 58, 59
      validator, 56, 57
   testing, 63
      Code Review Checklist, 70
      Creditcoin 1.8, 74
      creditcoin-legacy-tests, 67
      house-keeping transactions, 74
      Hyperledger Sawtooth framework, 68
      improvement on tests, 69–73
      integration test suite, 68
      programming languages, 69
      repositories, 66
      Sawtooth node, 68
      suspected networking issue, 74
      timeline, 62, 63
      CI enablement, 64–66
      repositories creation, 63, 64
Creditcoin 1.x client program, 46
Creditcoin 2
   cli test suite, 174
   repository, 169
   test suite, 172
Creditcoin 2.0, 61
   accounts/balance mappings, 80
   benchmarks, 86
   creditcoin-js library, 89, 191
   creditcoin-squid, 89, 90
   custom RPCs, 88
   extrinsics pallets
      creditcoin pallet, 83
      difficulty pallet, 84
      off-chain task scheduler pallet, 84
      rewards pallet, 84
   multi-threaded application, 81
   node, client and runtime, 81

INDEX

Creditcoin 2.0 (*cont.*)
    vs. 1.8 versions, 79
    pallets, 83
    protocol compatibility, 79
    reference hardware, 86
    replay program, 80
    RPC routing layer, 81
    runtime, 87, 88
    Rust programming language, 83
    storage migrations, 87, 88
    telemetry and custom
        metrics, 88, 89
    testing, 91
        "chaos" pallet, 122
        CI environment, 112
        creditcoin-squid, 120
        development and release
            process, 113–115
        Devnet environment, 112
        integration test, 98–102
        integration test and
            assert, 122
        Mainnet, 113
        migrations and upgrade
            testing, 106–112
        performance testing, 120
        Promise.all, 122
        sanity testing and static
            analysis, 102–104
        security-related testing,
            118, 119
        Testnet, 113
    testing with bots
        Dependabot, 104, 105
        Gluwa-bot, 105, 106
        pre-commit CI, 105
    timeline, 90, 91
    transaction fees, 85
    unit testing, 93–97
    weights, 86
Creditcoin 2.3, 125, 157
    components
        block history, 129
        creditcoin-cli, 127
        creditcoin-squid, 130
        Creditcoin Staking
            Dashboard, 129
        stock pallets, 126
        subscan essentials, 130
        switch_to_pos(), 127, 128
    creditcoin-cli, 148
    documentation, 190
    failures, 149
    security bounty program,
        148, 149
    testing
        challenges, 154–157
        community testing, 150
        Creditcoin-cli, 136, 137
        Creditcoin staking
            dashboard, 135, 136
        documentation, 144, 145
        gluwa/substrate, 138–140
        integration tests, 132, 133
        large-enough values, 152
        load/performance, 145–147
        load testing tools, 150
        migrations, 151

INDEX

OCW nonce, 153, 154
PoS, 149
PoW-PoS migration, 150
read/write operations, 152
staging environment, 153
stash and controller, 151
subscan essentials, 134
u32::MAX, 152
unit tests, 131
upgrade testing, 149
voting process, 154
testing objective, 131
timeline, 130
Creditcoin 3, 135, 163, 165, 167, 202
configuration, 172
development, 169
documentation, 190
testing, 206
Creditcoin 3.0, 48, 129, 136, 151, 159
challenges, 193, 194
block time, 195
layers and applications, 195
on-chain storage, 194
process, 195, 196
CJ jobs overview, 169
CLI integration test suite, 202
labels, 204
runners, 204
scenarios, 203
setup sections, 203
7000 workflow, 203
test jobs, 204
community interactions, 200
components
blockscout, 167
Creditcoin 3 CLI, 164
Crunch, 168
EVM tracing RPC, 162
frontier, 161, 162
polkadot-sdk, 160
precompiles, 163
proxy functionality, 164, 165
staking dashboard, 166
Subscan API, 167
design features, 159
documentation, 191
fast-runtime compiler flag, 186
GitHub interface, 205
integration-test-cli-entrypoint, 205
matrix jobs, 205
Polkadot JS Apps web interface, 193
proposal, 159
public announcement, 160
quality, 202
staking dashboard, 186
arbitrary, 189
CreditcoinLocal, 186
impacts, 188
issues, 187
non-development instance, 188
Polkadot, 187
SaaS, 188
staking page, 187
technical contribution, 186

INDEX

Creditcoin 3.0 (*cont.*)
  static files, 186
  testing, 168
    api variable, 181
    beforeAll/afterAll pair, 180
    blockchain instance, 180
    CLI commands, 177
    command line
      application, 176
    compiler warning, 192
    Creditcoin 3 CLI, 174, 175
    crunch, 190
    debugging, 183, 184
    EVM compatibility, 169
    EVM test suite, 170, 171
    EVM tracing, 171
    frontier, 189
    global.beforeEach, 181
    polkadot-sdk, 189
    precompiles, 173, 174
    proxy accounts, 175, 176
    proxy functionality, 175
    resource management,
      production environment,
      196, 198, 199
    runtime upgrade, 185
    setupFilesAfterEnv key, 180
    setup/teardown
      functions, 176
    shared state, 178, 179
    signatures, 179
    smart-contract test suite, 170
    startAliceAndBob
      function, 181
    TCP connections, 184
    test() and describe()
      functions, 176
    test files, 182
    testing combinations, 176
    test scenarios, 178
    *.test.ts files, 178
    transactions, 179
    unit testing, 169, 170
    validate.test.ts, 179
    validatorCycle.test.ts, 177
    variants, 177
  testing challenges, 206
  test jobs, 205
  test orchestrator, 200
  tests, 178
  timeline, 168
  traditional testing
    sequence, 199
  two-step approach, 201
Creditcoin blockchain
  canonical, open source
    implementation, 44
  credit-related activities, 46
  CTC, 46
  external artifacts, 46
  Initial Creditcoin
    implementation, 45
  loan-related transactions, 44
  loan terms, repayments and
    credit performance, 45
  real-world financial assets, 49
  schematic depiction, 44
  testing activities, 47–50

INDEX

transfer of assets, 45
Creditcoin chain, 45
Creditcoin-js, 89, 98, 104, 115, 191
creditcoin-legacy-docker-
    compose-testnet
    repository, 62, 64, 74
Creditcoin-legacy-shared, 71
Creditcoin-legacy-tests,
    61–62, 67, 80
Creditcoin loan cycle, 45, 213
Creditcoin PoS Testnet, 140
    community testing, 141
    CTC tokens, 140
    deployment
        blockchain, 143
        upgrading, 142, 143
Creditcoin-squid, 89, 90, 120, 130
CREDITCOIN
    transaction, 58, 60
Creditcoin transaction processors
    CREDITCOIN transaction, 58
    Sawtooth framework, 58
    settings-tp, 58
    versions 1.0 through 1.7, 59
Creditcoin v1.8, 75, 76
Crude CI enablement, 69
Cryptocurrencies, 3, 4, 6, 13,
    15–17, 45
Crypto faucet, 15
Crypto tokens, 13–16, 21, 22, 26, 27,
    45, 46, 116, 123, 125, 168
Cypress, 220
Cypress-polkadot-wallet, 221

D

Dappeteer, 222
Data availability, 217
Data immutability, 216
Data integrity, 6, 120
Data retention, 217
Decentralized blockchain, 3, 212
Dependabot, 67, 71, 104, 118, 119,
    134, 135, 168, 192
Devnet, 15, 112–117, 149, 186, 189
Distributed digital ledger, 5
Documentation
    Creditcoin 2.3, 144, 145
    Creditcoin 3.0, 191

E

End-to-end testing, 203, 219,
    222, 227
Engineers, 35, 49, 211, 214, 218, 219
Error handling, 89, 95, 97, 174, 176
Ethereum, 3, 8–10, 14, 16, 30, 31,
    34, 45, 60, 84, 123, 161,
    212, 226
Ethereum-compatible networks, 45
Ethereum ecosystem, 159
Ethereum Virtual Machine (EVM),
    17, 34, 159, 161–164,
    169–171, 190, 213, 221
ethers.js, 26, 174, 213, 228
EVM, *see* Ethereum Virtual
    Machine (EVM)
ExtBuilder, 95

INDEX

ExtBuilder::default().build_and_execute(), 95
Externalities builder, 95
Extrinsic functions, 83, 86, 93, 95, 103, 133

F

Faucet, 15
Fiat currency, 13, 45
Filecoin, 212
Finality, 8, 11, 216
Finalization, 11, 179
Forest, 212
Fork, 11, 57, 60, 61, 65, 67, 74, 75, 107, 130, 135, 138–140, 160, 167, 168, 187, 189, 190, 216

G

Ganache, 228
Gas or transaction fee, 9
Gateway, 60
Genesis block, 11, 58, 79, 108
Geth, 31
GitHub's CodeQL, 118
globalSetup value, 117
Gluwa-bot, 105–106
Goerli, 45, 226, 227
Goerli testnet, 123
Go programming language, 31, 130
Gossamer, 213

H

Hard forks, 11
Hash, 9, 10, 81, 132, 171
HEALTHCHECK command, 72
Hyperledger Caliper, 240
Hyperledger Sawtooth, 29–30, 38, 58, 68, 70, 75, 81
hyperledger/sawtooth-rest-api, 60
hyperledger/sawtooth-validator:1.0, 57
hyperledger/sawtooth-validator:1.2, 57

I

Integration testing, 98–102, 172, 178, 226
Integration tests, 68, 98, 101, 115, 116, 132–133, 173, 174
   block preservation, 132
   Creditcoin 2.3, 132, 133
   important items, 132
   smart contracts, 226
   upgrading, 133
Integration test suite, 68, 98, 101, 115, 122, 123, 132, 137, 171

J, K

Jest testing framework, 33, 98, 136, 172, 176

L

Linux operating system, 4
Load and performance testing, 145–147, 227
Lodestar, 212

M

Mainnet, 15, 79, 91, 108, 112–117, 122, 123, 137, 189
MegaLinter's Rust flavor, 119
MetaMask, 14, 214, 222, 223, 226
Migrations, 24, 80, 87–88, 106–112, 151, 157, 185, 194
Migration testing, 107–109, 115
Miners, 12, 27, 84, 88, 142–144
Mining, 12, 27, 84
Minters, 12
Multiple Sawtooth nodes, 53, 54
Multix, 214, 221

N

Native crypto token, 9, 46
Native token, 13
NFTs, *see* Non-fungible tokens (NFTs)
The NFT Marketplace, 224
  business requirements, 239
  code summary, 238
  costs, 228
  demonstration code, 229–233, 235–238
  entrypoint, testing, 228
  Ganache, 228
  Polygon, 225
  testing, 229
  Web 2.0 front-end, 224, 225
Nominated proof-of-stake (NPoS), 7, 125–128, 130, 131, 144, 145, 147, 149, 159, 168
Nominator, 13, 15, 125, 126, 129, 131, 140, 141, 144, 146, 166, 168
Nonce, 12, 122, 153, 154
Non-fungible tokens (NFTs), 217, 218, 223–226, 229, 238, 239
NPoS, *see* Nominated proof-of-stake (NPoS)

O

Object Relational Mapping framework, 23
OCW, *see* Off-chain workers (OCW)
Off-chain workers (OCW), 25, 60, 126, 153, 154
on_initialize(), 121, 151
Oracle, 25

P, Q

Peer-to-peer networking, 19, 81
Pinata, 218
Plan–Build–Test–Discover–Repeat, 49
PoA, *see* Proof of authority (PoA)

Polkadex, 187
Polkadot, 3, 30, 31, 49, 85, 86, 105, 123, 126, 135, 136, 145, 156, 187, 188, 213, 214, 221
polkadot-js-metadata-cmp tool, 103
Polkadot Network blockchain, 49
Polkadot/Parity Technologies, 49
Polkadot Wallet Snap for MetaMask, 214
Polygon zkEVM network, 17
PoS, *see* Proof-of-stake (PoS)
Postman, 228
PoW, *see* Proof of work (PoW)
PoW to PoS migration process, 150, 157
Pre-commit CI, 105, 134, 135
Programming languages, 16, 39, 69, 220
  Rust, 31–33
  Solidity, 34
  testing framework, 38
  TypeScript, 33
Proof of authority (PoA), 28
Proof-of-stake (PoS), 13, 15, 27–28, 125–127, 132, 137, 140–144, 147
Proof of work (PoW), 12, 26, 27, 57, 84, 126, 127, 129, 132, 133, 142, 144, 146, 157
Pyramid testing, 72, 220
Python, 30, 31, 48, 53, 57, 58, 98, 105
Python client library, 98

R

Reference hardware, 86, 106
RegisterDealOrder, 72
Remote procedure call (RPC) API, 22–23
REST API, 22, 26, 56, 59–60, 80
RestAssured library, 228
Rinkeby testnet, 123
RPC methods, 22, 88, 89, 162, 171
runtime/src/ directory, 86
Rust programming language, 31–33, 57, 93, 168, 192, 212

S

Sawtooth framework, 56, 58, 59, 63, 68
Sawtooth network diagram, 56
Sawtooth REST API, 80
Sawtooth-SDK-Cxx, 61
Sawtooth-SDK-Rust, 61
Security bounty program, 118, 147–149
Security-related testing, 118–119, 226
Sepolia, 45, 123, 227
Slashing, 15–16, 28
Smart-contract development tools, 159
Smart contracts, 6, 16, 17, 25, 26, 159, 161, 163, 170–171, 190, 198
  blockchain component, 240

definition, 223
end-to-end testing, 227
ethers.js, 228
integration testing, 226
load and performance testing, 227
NFTs, 224
presentation quote, 240
product under test
  digital content, 224
  users, 226
security-related testing, 226
testing strategy, 226, 227
NFT Marketplace (*see* The NFT Marketplace)
tools spectrum, 240
transitioning procedure, 239
unit testing, 226
Solidity, 16, 34, 163, 173
Stagenet, 15
Staked funds, 27
Staking, 15, 16, 126, 129, 166, 186, 197
Stash and controller concept, 151
Storage migrations, 87–88, 106–108, 115, 185, 194
Substrate API, 48
Substrate-based implementation, 38
Substrate blockchain framework, 24, 49, 81, 126
Substrate framework, 14, 35, 38, 81, 82, 86, 88, 97, 105, 119, 121, 123, 138, 147, 151, 160, 168

Substrate/Polkadot ecosystem, 33, 135, 187
SubWallet, 14, 129, 166
switch_to_pos(), 127–128, 132, 150, 157
Sygma, 213, 219

T

Testers, 6, 15, 32, 35, 156, 202, 210, 228, 240
Testing framework, 33, 38, 93, 98, 172, 176, 220
Testing tools, 48, 150, 214, 220, 221
Testnet, 15, 48, 108, 112–116, 122, 133, 140–144, 150, 168, 186, 220
TestWarez testing conference, 239
Third-party tools, 190–192
time.set transaction, 21
Traditional banking system, 43
Transaction business logic, 30
Transaction families, 30, 58, 61, 68
Transaction fees, 9, 21, 22, 47, 85, 86, 103, 122, 137
Transaction hash, 9, 16
Transactions, 7–10, 12, 14–16, 20–21, 24, 81, 122, 147, 162, 167, 170, 171
Transaction schema, 20
TypeScript, 33, 48, 133, 172
TypeScript client libraries, 133

U

Unit testing, 93–97, 131, 136, 139, 170–171
  Creditcoin 2.3, 131
  Creditcoin 3.0, 169, 170
  smart contracts, 226
Upgrade testing, 107–112
Utility token, 13, 46

V

Validator component, 56–58
Validators, 12, 13, 16, 21, 56–57, 125, 126, 144, 146, 179
Virtual machines, 17, 86, 197, 204

W, X, Y

Wallet address, 14, 15
Wallet apps, 14, 159
WASM, *see* WebAssembly (WASM)
Web3, 16, 45, 145, 148, 187
web3.js, 213
web3.unity, 213
WebAssembly (WASM), 24, 87, 88, 114, 115, 119, 133
WebSocket, 22, 88, 127

Z

ZeroMQ, 23, 59, 60
Zombienet, 146, 147

GPSR Compliance

The European Union's (EU) General Product Safety Regulation (GPSR) is a set of rules that requires consumer products to be safe and our obligations to ensure this.

If you have any concerns about our products, you can contact us on

ProductSafety@springernature.com

In case Publisher is established outside the EU, the EU authorized representative is:

Springer Nature Customer Service Center GmbH
Europaplatz 3
69115 Heidelberg, Germany

www.ingramcontent.com/pod-product-compliance
Lightning Source LLC
LaVergne TN
LVHW010338260326
834688LV00036B/775